Hazardous Waste Management in Small Businesses

Recent Titles from Quorum Books

Pollution Law Handbook: A Guide to Federal Environmental Laws
Sidney M. Wolf

Hazardous Waste: Confronting the Challenge
Christopher Harris, William L. Want, and Morris A. Ward, with the Environmental Law Institute

A Guide to Hazardous Materials Management: Physical Characteristics, Federal Regulations, and Response Alternatives
Aileen Schumacher

America's Future in Toxic Waste Management: Lessons from Europe
Bruce Piasecki

Chemical Contamination and Its Victims: Medical Remedies, Legal Redress, and Public Policy
David W. Schnare and Martin T. Katzman, editors

Environmentally Induced Cancer and the Law: Risks, Regulation, and Victim Compensation
Frank B. Cross

Financial Futures and Options: A Guide to Markets, Applications, and Strategies
Todd E. Petzel

Problem Employees and Their Personalities: A Guide to Behaviors, Dynamics, and Intervention Strategies for Personnel Specialists
William T. Martin

The Banking System in Troubled Times: New Issues of Stability and Continuity
Jeremy F. Taylor

Real Interest Rates and Investment Borrowing Strategy
Peter S. Spiro

The Political Limits of Environmental Regulation: Tracking the Unicorn
Bruce Yandle

Summary Judgment and Other Preclusive Devices
Warren Freedman

Distinction Between Measurement and Interpretation in Accounting: A Living Systems Theory Approach
G. A. Swanson and James Grier Miller

Hazardous Waste Management In Small Businesses

Regulating and Assisting the Smaller Generator

Robert E. Deyle

Q

QUORUM BOOKS
New York • Westport, Connecticut • London

Library of Congress Cataloging-in-Publication Data

Deyle, Robert E.
  Hazardous waste management in small businesses : regulating and
assisting the smaller generator / Robert E. Deyle.
     p. cm.
  Bibliography: p.
  Includes index.
  ISBN 0–89930–349–8 (lib. bdg. : alk. paper)
  1. Hazardous wastes—Management.   2. Small business—Waste
disposal.   3. Liability for hazardous substances pollution damages.
I. Title.
TD1030.D49   1989   89–32859

British Library Cataloguing in Publication Data is available.

Library of Congress Catalog Card Number: 89–32859
ISBN: 0–89930–349–8

First published in 1989 by Quorum Books

Greenwood Press, Inc.
88 Post Road West, Westport, Connecticut 06881

Printed in the United States of America

The paper used in this book complies with the
Permanent Paper Standard issued by the National
Information Standards Organization (Z39.48-1984).

10 9 8 7 6 5 4 3 2 1

To Trudy

Contents

viii Contents

Tables

Acknowledgments

Several people are deserving of particular thanks for their roles in the successful completion of this endeavor. Steve Ballard, director of the Science and Public Policy Program at the University of Oklahoma, and the other faculty members of the program were very generous in their personal support and forbearance while this book was in preparation. Lennet Bledsoe, Carol Bernstein, and Eileen Hasselwander of the Science and Public Policy staff are due great thanks for their patience and diligence in assisting in the preparation of the manuscript.

The design and implementation of the survey of smaller generators in New Jersey was accomplished while I was a research associate with the Technology and Information Policy Program at Syracuse University. Barry Bozeman, director of the program, provided personal encouragement, intellectual guidance, and the resources of the program, all of which were essential to the success of the project. I am also indebted to my other intellectual mentors and advisors at the State University of New York College of Environmental Science and Forestry and Syracuse University, including Stuart Bretschneider, Linda Fowler, Paul Graves, and Susan Long.

The New Jersey survey was funded through a contract between Syracuse University and the New Jersey Hazardous Waste Facilities Siting Commission. Susan Boyle, assistant director of the commission, deserves recognition for her appreciation of the intellectual value of the policy issues facing the commission and for her patience and professionalism in working with an academic contractor. Rosemary O'Leary, a contributor to this book, is owed immense thanks for her contribution and her tireless efforts as project director of the New Jersey study while at Syracuse University.

Finally I owe a debt of immeasurable dimension to my family for their support and love throughout the four years during which this endeavor has occupied my time and energy. To my wife, Trudy, and my children, Anna and Ethan, I express my deepest gratitude and devotion.

Abbreviations

ABAG	Association of Bay Area Governments
AICPA	American Institute of Certified Public Accountants
CHMR	Center for Hazardous Materials Research
CERCLA	Comprehensive Environmental Response Compensation and Liability Act
CFR	Code of Federal Regulations
DEC	Department of Environmental Conservation
DOL	Department of Labor
EFC	Environmental Facilities Corporation
EPA	Environmental Protection Agency
EPASBO	Environmental Protection Agency, Small Business Ombudsman
ERM	Environmental Resources Management, Inc.
FDER	Florida Department of Environmental Regulation
FTC	Federal Trade Commission
GAO	Government Accounting Office
GRCDA	Governmental Refuse Collection and Disposal Association
HSWA	Hazardous and Solid Waste Amendments
kg	kilograms

kg/mo	kilograms/month
NTSB	National Transportation Safety Board
OSHA	Occupational Safety and Health Act
OTA	Office of Technology Assessment
PRP	Potentially Responsible Party
RCRA	Resource Conservation and Recovery Act
RITTA	RCRA Integrated Training and Technical Assistance
SBANE	Smaller Business Association of New England
SBTG	Environmental Protection Agency Small Business Task Group
SIC	Standard Industrial Classification
SQG	Small Quantity Generator
SVC	Small Volume Contributor
TIPP	Technology and Information Policy Program
TSDF	Treatment Storage and Disposal Facility
USCOC	United States Chamber of Commerce
VSQG	Very Small Quantity Generator

1

The Smaller Generator
Challenge

Small businesses that generate hazardous wastes as byproducts of the services and products they sell present a significant public policy challenge. Although they produce a minor proportion of all the hazardous wastes generated in the United States, smaller generators are more likely to mismanage their wastes than larger businesses. Furthermore, mismanagement of small amounts of some hazardous wastes can present substantial threats to public safety and environmental quality.

The population of smaller generators is vast in number and more transient than larger, regulated firms. They produce a great diversity of products and services and consequently produce a wide array of hazardous wastes. Most smaller generators have limited technical expertise in waste management and limited experience with regulations as complex as those governing hazardous wastes. Small-business decision makers typically have little time to devote to fully understanding applicable regulations and are reluctant to invest in engineering or legal expertise that does not contribute to production of goods or services.

The policy questions at issue concern how government can most effectively minimize threats to public health and the environment from hazardous waste produced by smaller generators. Direct federal and state regulation was extended over a portion of the smaller generator population by the 1984 Hazardous and Solid Waste Amendments. This policy initiative relies on the traditional command-and-control regulatory approach to achieve desired changes in behavior. It is based on the assumption that the threat of inspections and sanctions will induce small quantity generators to manage their wastes in conformance with specified procedures. Recognition of some of the constraints on regulatory compliance by smaller generators led policy makers to supplement this regulatory strategy with educational programs and technical and financial assistance initiatives. While the initial focus of these programs was on compliance assistance, there has been a shift in emphasis in recent years to promoting more advanced waste management practices by smaller generators, such as source reduction and recycling.

Questions remain as to the impact these recent policy initiatives are likely to have. How effective can we expect command-and-control regulations to be in motivating decision makers in smaller generator businesses to manage their hazardous wastes properly? To what extent can education and assistance programs initiated by the public sector contend with the constraints on regulatory compliance that are peculiar to smaller businesses? To what degree should public resources be targeted at enhancing compliance by smaller generators with minimum waste management standards versus promoting more advanced waste management practices?

This book examines these policy questions based on recent studies of hazardous waste management and compliance behavior of smaller generators and evaluations of smaller generator assistance programs. Background information characterizing smaller generators, their hazardous wastes, and waste management practices is presented in this chapter to define the context of these policy issues. Chapter 2 assesses the options available to government for influencing private-sector environmental management and examines decisionmaking by small businesses. Chapter 3 examines the compliance theory that underlies environmental regulatory programs, reviews the evidence from studies of individual and corporate compliance behavior, and assesses the implications for influencing compliance by small businesses. In Chapter 4, Rosemary O'Leary discusses the liability exposure of small businesses that generate hazardous wastes and the implications of liability for the smaller generator's waste management practices. Chapter 5 reviews the findings of several studies of compliance with hazardous waste regulations and presents the results of an analysis by the author of adherence by smaller generators to hazardous waste regulations in New Jersey. Chapter 6 concludes with an assessment of federal and state programs that have been undertaken to enhance hazardous waste management by smaller generators.

DEFINING SMALLER GENERATORS

Smaller generators include two groups of establishments that produce hazardous waste: those subject to federal and state regulation and those that are exempt from most of the regulatory requirements. Prior to the federal Hazardous and Solid Waste Amendments of 1984 (HSWA), such a distinction was not necessary, except in a few states. Under the 1976 Resource Conservation and Recovery Act (RCRA), all establishments that generated less than 1,000 kilograms of hazardous waste in a calendar month (kg/mo) were exempt from most of the federal regulations governing the "large quantity" generators that produced 1,000 or more kg/mo of hazardous waste. These so-called conditionally exempt generators were also collectively referred to as "small quantity generators" or SQGs.

The 1984 amendments extended federal regulation to generators of between 100 and 1,000 kg/mo. Thus a distinction is now made in the Code of Federal Regulations (CFR) between small quantity generators (SQGs) in the 100 to 1,000 kg/mo range and the remaining conditionally exempt or "very small quantity" generators (VSQGs) that produce less than 100 kg/mo (40 CFR 261.5). The SQGs and VSQGs are collectively referred to here as "smaller generators" to differentiate them from the large quantity generators.

The smaller generators include about 440,000 manufacturing, service, and retail businesses and public institutions, from over 200 Standard Industrial Classification (SIC) codes (Abt Associates, Inc. 1983; Ruder et al. 1985: 47). Approximately 90,000 of these establishments are estimated to qualify as regulated SQGs, while the remaining 350,000 establishments are conditionally exempt VSQGs.

As shown in Table 1.1, the five major industry groups, based on waste volumes, include the following:

1. metal manufacturing (plating and metal fabrication shops)
2. vehicle maintenance (automotive repair and body shops)
3. printing and ceramics firms
4. photography firms
5. laundries (dry cleaners and commercial laundries).

When ranked by numbers of firms, the pesticide application services group replaces photography in the top five industry groups.

Most smaller generators are also small businesses based on the commonly used metric of number of employees: nationally 67 percent have fewer than 50 employees and 78 percent have fewer than 100 employees (Klosky et al. 1985: 5.3). There are, however, some smaller generators that are relatively large firms. Data from a 1985 survey of smaller generators in New Jersey illustrate this disparity. While the average firm size in the survey was fifty-eight employees, the median was eighteen. Seventy-five percent of the firms had fifty or fewer employees, yet the five largest firms ranged in size from 300 to 2,000 employees.

Table 1.1
Smaller Generator Industry Groups Ranked by Annual Waste Volume

Industry Group	Annual Waste (MT/yr)[*]
Metal Manufacturing	64,652
Vehicle Maintenance	60,092
Printing/Ceramics	18,307
Photography	18,052
Laundries	13,418
Other Services	10,706
Pesticide Application Services	8,444
Analytical & Clinical Laboratories	7,171
Other Manufacturing	5,361
Construction	5,033
Wholesale and Retail Trades	3,876
Furniture/Wood Manufacture & Refinishing	3,703
Chemical Manufacturing	2,373
Formulators	2,333
Cleaning Agents & Cosmetics Manufacturers	1,569
Educational & Vocational Shops	1,179
Pesticide End Users	1,122
Equipment Repair	943
Wood Preserving	715
Textile Manufacturing	650
Paper Industry	544
Motor Freight Terminals	161

[*]Excluding lead-acid batteries.

Source: Ruder et al. (1985: D-3).

Many smaller generators lack sufficient understanding of the nature of hazardous wastes, how they are generated, and how they should be managed. In many instances, smaller generators are not aware of or do not understand the applicable hazardous waste regulations (Finegan 1986: 65–66). Most smaller generators are also not subject to other federal and state environmental regulations and therefore have little experience with the legal and technical aspects of such programs (Jones 1984: 3).

Environmental regulations in general, and hazardous waste regulations in particular, present complex legal and technical issues that are particularly difficult for small businesses. Lane (1966: 96) found that many small-business executives reported having difficulty keeping current with laws and regulations in the mid–1960s when most of the current environmental and health and safety regulations did not exist. Data from recent studies support the assumption that small businesses have insufficient time, money, and expertise to fully comply with environmental regulations. Studies of small business understanding of environmental and hazardous waste regulations also indicate that knowledge is likely to be a significant constraint on regulatory compliance (SBANE 1983: 1; Steger et al. 1983: 2.31, 2.43–2.48, 2.59–60; Deyle 1985: 32; ERM 1985: 31; USCOC 1982).

Smaller businesses typically have fewer financial resources to invest in staff devoted to nonproductive functions such as waste management and regulatory compliance (Deyle 1985: 32; Sloan et al. 1983: 294; Sommers and Cole 1981: 26). Companies with fewer than 100 employees are less able to afford an engineer who can stay abreast of regulations and interpret and implement them (Steger et al. 1983: 2.33). Smaller businesses are also less likely to hire engineering or legal consultants to assist in determining how environmental regulations apply to them or in solving technological problems of regulatory compliance (Steger et al. 1983: 2.8, 2.18).

A 1984 survey of 100 SQGs in North Carolina found that the majority of decisions concerning hazardous waste management were made by firm presidents, owners, or general managers (Wu et al. 1984: 22). In the New Jersey study, firm owners had primary responsibility for hazardous waste management in 35 percent of the businesses surveyed, while other upper level managers were responsible in an additional 27 percent. Hazardous waste management was dealt with by an operating manager or engineer in only 29 percent of the firms (Bozeman et al. 1986b: 73). Only 22 percent of the New Jersey waste management decision makers had access to in-house environmental managers or engineers, while 41 percent made use of environmental consultants for advice on waste management (Bozeman et al. 1986b: 91). The advice of legal consultants was employed by 28 percent of the firms in making decisions concerning waste management.

SMALLER GENERATOR WASTE MANAGEMENT

An understanding of the principal hazardous wastes produced by smaller generators and the waste management practices employed by them is essential to assessing the importance of public-sector initiatives to influence their waste management practices. This section describes the hazardous wastes produced by smaller generators and how those waste streams are managed.

In the aggregate, smaller generators rely to a greater extent on commercial facilities located offsite for waste treatment, recycling, and disposal than managing wastes themselves on the same sites as their production facilities. Analysis of data generated from a 1985 national survey of smaller generators indicates that approximately 60 percent of all smaller generators ship some of their wastes offsite, while 54 percent treat, recycle, or dispose of some of their wastes onsite.[1] Reliance on offsite management is more evident when comparisons are made in terms of waste volumes: approximately 60 percent of the hazardous wastes produced by smaller generators is treated, recycled, or disposed of at offsite facilities, while 40 percent is managed onsite. If wastes discharged to public sewer systems and septic tanks are removed from the total, the split is much greater: 76 percent managed offsite versus 23 percent onsite.

The 1985 national survey data indicate that 12 percent of smaller generators were employing some onsite recycling of hazardous wastes at that time, and 23 percent were utilizing commercial recycling services located offsite. Twenty-five percent were disposing of hazardous wastes in sanitary landfills, either onsite or offsite, while only 4 percent were using land disposal facilities permitted for hazardous wastes. Thirty-two percent of smaller generators were disposing of hazardous wastes in public sewers or septic tanks. This practice accounted for approximately 23 percent of all hazardous waste produced by smaller generators. Only about 3 percent employed solid waste incinerators for disposal, while 2 percent used incinerators permitted for hazardous wastes.

Table 1.2 lists the ten major categories of hazardous wastes produced by smaller generators. Spent solvents predominate. These include cleaning, degreasing, and stripping solvents used in metal working and plating shops, vehicle maintenance, equipment repair, and construction, as well as solvents used in cleaning printing presses (CHMR 1987; Phifer and McTigue 1988; Ruder et al. 1985; EPA 1985). Results of the 1985 national survey indicate that 12 percent of smaller generators discharge spent solvents to sewer systems or septic tanks (Ruder et al. 1985: E–7–8). Ten percent use sufficient quantities of solvents to make it cost-effective to recycle onsite (CHMR 1987: 9–2; Schwartz et al. 1987: 86). Most smaller generators, however, contract with waste haulers or waste management

Table 1.2
Major Hazardous Wastes Produced by Smaller Generators*

Waste Type	Annual Waste (MT/yr)
Spent Solvents	105,368
Strong Acids or Alkalies	29,791
Photographic Wastes	18,431
Dry Cleaning Filtration Residues	13,660
Solutions or Sludges Containing Silver	8,919
Waste Formaldehyde	8,850
Ignitable Wastes	8,485
Ignitable Paint Wastes	6,713
Pesticide Solutions	6,069
Spent Plating Wastes	5,768

*Excluding lead-acid batteries.

Source: Ruder et al. (1985: 38).

firms to collect spent solvents for disposal or recycling at facilities located offsite. Ten percent ship offsite to sanitary landfills, and 6 percent ship offsite to hazardous waste landfills or incinerators. Some have contracts with solvent suppliers to collect and recycle used solvents. Overall, 33 percent ship spent solvents offsite for recycling.

Strong acids and alkalies are principally generated from metal parts cleaning and rust removal in vehicle maintenance shops, preparation of printing plates, pickling solutions used in metal plating, and wastes from analytic and clinical laboratories. Most of these wastes are highly dilute and are frequently discharged to public sewer systems with or without pretreatment to neutralize the pH (CHMR 1987: 7–11). The 1985 national survey indicated that 40 percent of smaller generators discharge strong acid and alkali wastes to sewers or septic systems, while only 12 percent neutralize these wastes prior to discharge (Ruder et al. 1985: E–8–9). Fourteen percent recycle or reuse these wastes onsite, while 10 percent ship acid and alkali wastes offsite for recycling. Eight percent of smaller generators were estimated to be disposing of these wastes offsite in sanitary landfills, while only 3 percent were using commercial landfill facilities permitted for hazardous wastes.

Solutions and sludges containing silver and other photographic wastes are generated by the printing industry as well as the photographic industry. These wastes include spent fix-processing solutions, developers, ferricyanide bleach, and bleach-fix solutions (CHMR 1987: 8.7–1). Seventy-seven percent of smaller generators discharge these wastes to sewer or septic tank systems (Ruder et al. 1985: E–10). Silver is typically recovered from spent fix solutions and, less frequently, from other photographic wastes. The recycling of bleaches onsite is also becoming more common. Federal and state regulations requiring pretreatment of industrial wastewater prior to discharge to public sewers have been a major stimulus to recovering both silver and bleach. Waste formaldehyde, which is produced almost entirely by funeral establishments, is also principally discharged to public sewer systems (Ruder et al. 1985: 38).

Dry cleaning filtration residues include still residues from perchloroethylene, Valclene, and petroleum solvent distillation systems and spent filter cartridges from perchloroethylene and Valclene plants (EPA 1985). Dry cleaning establishments without solvent recovery systems onsite return solvents to the supplier or ship spent solvents offsite to a solvent reclaimer (CHMR 1987: 8.5–5).

Ignitable paint wastes include those containing flammable thinners or reducers in sufficient quantity to have a flashpoint of less than 140 degrees Fahrenheit (EPA 1985). These are produced primarily from construction activities, furniture manufacturing and refinishing, metal manufacturing, and vehicle maintenance shops. The majority of smaller generators (52 percent) dispose of these wastes in sanitary landfills, either offsite or onsite (Ruder et al. 1985: E–13). Only about 19 percent recycle these wastes onsite or ship them to offsite recycling facilities. Approximately 17 percent of the smaller generators dispose of ignitable paint wastes in public sewer systems or septic tanks.

The "other ignitable wastes" category includes liquids with a flashpoint of less than 140 degrees Fahrenheit, solids that ignite spontaneously, flammable gases, and oxidizers (EPA 1985). The major other ignitable wastes produced by smaller generators include the following: carburetor and engine cleaners; petroleum distillates; paint thinners, alcohols, and mineral spirits; paint and varnish removers; epoxy resins and adhesives; rags containing flammable solvents and degreasers; and spent reagents and cleaning solutions from analytic and clinical laboratories. These are produced primarily in the vehicle maintenance, metal manufacturing, construction, and furniture manufacturing and refinishing industries in addition to analytic and clinical labs. In 1985, 35 percent of smaller generators were estimated to be shipping these wastes to sanitary landfills for disposal (Ruder et al. 1985: E–14–15). Fifteen percent shipped ignitable wastes offsite for recycling, while only 4 percent recycled such wastes onsite. Seventeen percent discharged ignitable wastes to public sewers or septic tank systems.

Pesticide solutions include dilute pesticide rinses generated by pesticide end-users and pesticide application services from cleaning equipment and containers. Farmers who use pesticides are exempt from most federal hazardous waste regulations if pesticide containers are triple rinsed and the rinse solutions are used or disposed of on the farmer's property in accordance with pesticide label instructions (EPA 1985). Most waste pesticide solutions disposed of by other pesticide end-users and application services are discharged to sewer systems or septic tanks or applied to land (Ruder et al. 1985: D–5).

Spent plating wastes are generated by the metal electroplating industry and from the manufacture of printing plates and cylinders. Acid plating solutions contain free acids and heavy metals including cadmium, chromium, copper, nickel, tin, and zinc. Alkaline plating baths primarily include tin and zinc. The waste products include spent plating bath solutions and sludges as well as stripping and cleaning bath solutions (Ruder et al. 1985; EPA 1985). Most waste plating solutions are discharged to municipal sewer systems following pretreatment to adjust pH and remove heavy metals. The resulting heavy metal sludges are disposed of primarily at landfills located offsite (CHMR 1987: 8.3–2). Cyanide wastes, which are also generated from metal plating operations, are categorized separately because of their high toxicity and specialized treatment and disposal requirements. Cyanide wastes are produced in significantly smaller quantities than other plating wastes. The 1985 national survey estimated annual production by smaller generators at about 2,100 metric tons per year (Ruder et al. 1985: 38).

REGULATION OF SMALLER GENERATORS

Most of the federal regulations governing SQG waste management went into effect on September 22, 1986. They essentially require SQGs to comply with the same requirements that formerly applied only to large quantity generators, with some exceptions. SQGs are required to determine if wastes they generate qualify as hazardous wastes (40 CFR 262.11), and they must obtain an EPA identification number (40 CFR 262.12). They must only treat or dispose of hazardous wastes in facilities with federal hazardous waste permits, and they must utilize a federal or state uniform manifest to track shipments of hazardous wastes to offsite facilities for treatment, storage, or disposal (40 CFR 262.20–23). SQGs must also comply with EPA and federal Department of Transportation requirements for marking and labeling hazardous waste containers (40 CFR 262.31–32 and 49 CFR 172).

SQGs are granted some reductions, however, in regulatory requirements compared to the large quantity generators. They are permitted to store hazardous wastes onsite prior to shipment to an offsite treatment, storage, or disposal facility for longer periods of time than are large quantity generators without obtaining a permit for hazardous waste storage (40 CFR 262.34[d]). SQGs are also subject to less comprehensive reporting requirements than large quantity generators (40 CFR 262.40–262.44). When a SQG sends waste to an offsite facility for reclamation and subsequently uses regenerated material from the reclaimer, a manifest is not necessitated provided certain requirements are met in the contractual agreement between the SQG and the reclaimer (40 CFR 262.20). SQGs also are not required to meet the detailed requirements for employee training, accident preparedness and prevention, and development of written accident contingency plans (40 CFR 265.16, subparts C and D). SQGs are only required to have a designated emergency coordinator and must assure that all employees are familiar with proper waste handling and emergency procedures (40 CFR 262.34(d)).

VSQGs are subject to federal regulation only under limited circumstances: when they generate one or more kg/mo of several specific wastes defined as acutely hazardous, when 100 kg or more of material contaminated by an acutely hazardous waste is produced as the result of a spill or leak, or when they accumulate more than 100 kg of hazardous waste onsite or any of the above-defined quantities of acutely hazardous waste within a calendar month (40 CFR 261.5).

Prior to HSWA, twenty-five states employed the 1,000 kg/mo threshold but did subject small quantity generators to some lesser regulatory requirements. Eleven other states regulated generators of between 1,000 kg/mo and some lower threshold ranging from 200 to 1 kg/mo, while five states had no lower bound to regulation (GAO 1983: 11). A recent review of state regulations governing smaller generators indicates that eight states have lower thresholds than the federal criteria for conditionally exempt VSQGs or more stringent regulations for VSQGs or SQGs (Phifer and McTigue 1988: 146–53). These states include California, Kansas, Louisiana, Minnesota, New Jersey, North Carolina, Rhode Island, and South Carolina. In New Jersey, SQGs have been subject since 1981 to the same regulations as large quantity generators.

IMPORTANCE OF IMPROVING SMALLER GENERATOR WASTE MANAGEMENT

The SQGs and VSQGs generate only about 0.4 percent of the total volume of hazardous wastes produced in the nation (Ruder et al. 1985:

27–28). While earlier assessments concluded that the health and safety impacts of not regulating these wastes would be minimal (Ghassemi et al. 1979; 1980), more recent studies have concluded that mismanagement of even small quantities of many types of hazardous waste can significantly impact local public health and the environment (Industrial Economics, Inc. 1985: 1.8–1.9; Jones and Fax 1984a: 2–3; Klosky et al. 1985: 1.3; SBTG 1984: 2).

In some states smaller generators may generate a significantly higher proportion of total hazardous wastes, or they may be the primary source of specific waste types. In Massachusetts, for instance, smaller generators are reported to be responsible for the production of 25 percent of the state's regulated hazardous wastes (OTA 1986: 209). In Florida, smaller generators are estimated to account for about 19 percent of the hazardous wastes produced by businesses and institutions (FDER 1988).

A 1983 study by the federal General Accounting Office (GAO) identified a number of specific concerns associated with improper management of hazardous wastes produced by smaller generators (GAO 1983: 14, 18, 19):

1. disposal of liquid hazardous wastes in municipal sewer systems;
2. occupational health and safety problems resulting from the disposal of hazardous wastes in sanitary landfills rather than in facilities designed specifically for managing hazardous wastes;
3. groundwater contamination resulting from disposal of hazardous wastes in sanitary landfills.

Adequacy of Current Waste Management Practices

The findings of the 1985 national survey concerning waste management practices by smaller generators support the concerns raised by the GAO. Studies of smaller generator waste management practices by states and local governments also indicate that a significant proportion of hazardous wastes produced by smaller generators are not being managed properly.

The national survey of smaller generators provides some rough figures on voluntary adherence with manifest and container labeling requirements by both regulated SQGs and conditionally exempt VSQGs. Only 6 percent of the respondents to the national survey who shipped hazardous wastes offsite indicated that they used a federal manifest, and only 25 percent reported that they used any kind of container label (Ruder et al. 1985: 46). No data were collected to determine the extent to which container labeling was done in conformance with federal regulatory requirements. Analyses of SQG hazardous waste management practices in New Jersey indicate that from 27 to 47 percent may be operating entirely outside state regulatory programs (Bozeman et al. 1986a: 119; Jones and

Fax 1984a: 10). Voluntary adherence to hazardous waste regulations by VSQGs in New Jersey has been estimated to be as low as 1 to 2 percent (Bozeman et al. 1986a: 119). Estimated noncompliance rates varied considerably among industry groups and individual SIC codes, with a range from almost 0 to as high as 90 percent.

In Florida it was determined that only 35 percent of the hazardous wastes produced by smaller generators were being managed properly in 1984 (FDER 1988: 3). A 1984 survey of smaller generators conducted by the Association of Bay Area Governments in the San Francisco Bay area found that 57 percent of the businesses surveyed were mismanaging some of their hazardous wastes (Russell and Meiorin 1985: IV–75). Violations included disposing of hazardous waste in municipal landfills; dumping it in sewers, on the ground, or in unlined ponds; or storing wastes for indeterminate periods of time. Another survey conducted by the Southern California Association of Governments in 1985 determined that as much as 20 percent of liquid hazardous wastes had been improperly managed by SQGs (Schwartz et al. 1987: 15). A study conducted in Massachusetts in 1986 estimated that only about 36 percent of autobody shops were in compliance with state regulations requiring generators to obtain federal EPA identification numbers if they generated more than 20 kilograms per month of solvents or waste oils (Brown et al. 1988: 1345).

Rebovich (1986) reviewed seventy-one completed hazardous waste criminal cases in four states: Maine, Maryland, New Jersey, and Pennsylvania. All but Maine have high levels of known hazardous waste criminal offenses, and all four states have well-developed environmental enforcement programs. He found that generators as a group were the largest single category of prosecuted firms (twenty-seven out of seventy-one), although the distributions varied among the states, in large part due to differences in enforcement targeting.

Generators with between one and fifty employees accounted for the majority of criminal cases in the four states. Rebovich suggests that the simpler organizational structures and more centralized decisionmaking of these smaller firms may account for the significant amount of criminal involvement by upper management. He also notes that smaller firms may predominate in the sample because of the greater ease of detection and greater prosecution success rates.

Nemeth and Kamperman (1985) report the results of a waste management review and auditing program conducted by Georgia Tech for SQGs from September 1983 through August 1984. A total of 56 onsite visits were made, to businesses of which 61 percent had 100 or fewer employees, and 78 percent had 200 or fewer. Nemeth and Kamperman state that most of the compliance problems they encountered involved waste container labeling, or waste disposal or storage practices, including storing wastes onsite beyond the then specified ninety-day limit and dumping

Table 1.3
Noncompliance Frequencies for SQGs in the 1985 Georgia Tech Onsite Consultation Program

Noncompliant Action	Frequency	Percentage
Lack of generator identification number	10/106	9
Violation of storage regulations	28/106	26
Failure to utilize manifest	13/106	12
Improper container labeling	24/106	23

Source: Nemeth and Kamperman (1986: 3, 6).

wastes in parking lots, backlots, sewer systems, or sanitary landfills via dumpsters. Data presented in the 1985 Final Report of the Georgia Tech OnSite Consultation Program, summarized in Table 1.3, offer some perspective on the extent of noncompliance encountered among firms with 200 or fewer employees over a two-year period. It is likely that these figures under estimate the actual rates of noncompliance, however, since participation in the Georgia Tech consultation program was entirely voluntary.

Similar results were reported from a pilot project conducted by the New York State Environmental Facilities Corporation in 1986 and 1987 that involved onsite waste management audits of SQGs. Regulatory violations included improper container labeling, illegal waste disposal practices, and failure to obtain EPA identification numbers (Snow 1988b). Other voluntary waste audit programs have found that most SQGs are not in full compliance with the regulations even when managers are aware of the regulations and the fact that they are subject to them. In the onsite consultation program recently initiated by the Center for Hazardous Materials Research (CHMR) at the University of Pittsburgh, 100 percent of the firms visited were out of compliance to some extent (Katz 1988: 65). The CHMR staff found SQGs that remained unaware of the applicability of hazardous waste laws to their firms and "many that still don't want to accept that fact" (Katz 1988: 68).

Overall there appears to be a consensus at federal and state levels that control of smaller generator waste management deserves greater attention than would be apparent from merely considering the absolute quantities of hazardous wastes produced by these establishments. This concern is reflected in a variety of policy initiatives:

1. identification and assessment of smaller generator populations through surveys or extrapolations from the 1985 national survey;
2. creation of education and technical assistance programs;
3. provision of transfer stations and collection route services to decrease transportation costs;
4. development of financial incentive and assistance programs to enhance hazardous waste management at smaller generator businesses.

These initiatives to enhance hazardous waste management by smaller generators are discussed in detail in Chapter 6.

CONCLUSIONS

There is a consensus that mismanagement of hazardous wastes by smaller generators poses a threat to public health and the environment of significant magnitude to justify the expenditure of public resources. State and federal officials also recognize that strict reliance on a command-and-control regulatory approach may be inadequate given the likely constraints on compliance posed by the limited resources and expertise of most small businesses. The next two chapters provide the background for assessing the policy options available to federal and state governments for influencing hazardous waste management by smaller generators given the characteristics of small businesses and their decisionmaking processes.

NOTE

1. Statistics for smaller generator waste management practices are derived from Appendix D of Ruder et al. (1985). Adjustments have been made to exclude lead-acid batteries, which were included as a hazardous waste in the 1985 national survey but are not regulated as such by the federal government or most states. Data in Appendix E of the report were used along with the assumption that 96 percent of all generators of lead-acid batteries do not generate other wastes that qualify as regulated hazardous wastes (Ruder et al. 1985: 47).

2

Influencing Environmental Management by Small Businesses

Policies employed to influence private-sector actions that affect environmental quality are based on concepts of decisionmaking and behavior principally attributable to large businesses and corporations. When the behavior of small businesses is of concern, public initiatives should reflect pertinent differences in the decisionmaking processes of large and small businesses. This chapter begins with a review of the alternatives that have been proposed or used to influence environmental management by establishments in the private sector. I then examine models of organizational decisionmaking and how they apply to small businesses and their environmental management behavior. The chapter concludes with a review of empirical data on small business decisionmaking and a discussion of the implications for influencing small-business actions that may affect the environment.

INFLUENCING PRIVATE-SECTOR ENVIRONMENTAL MANAGEMENT

Economists argue against intervention in transactions by the private sector except when market failures inhibit attaining social goals of efficiency or equity. Society has justified its intervention in private-sector actions that affect environmental quality because of a class of market failures called externalities. Externalities are actions that result in costs or benefits accruing to individuals not directly involved in the action.

When the externality results in benefits to a person who is not directly involved in a transaction, the externality is "positive." Government intervention in private-sector environmental management is directed at "negative" externalities when private-sector actions impose costs, in the form of impairment of environmental quality or public health.

Hazardous waste generation can result in externality costs. Hazardous wastes are environmental residuals. They are nonproduct outputs, the value of which is less than the costs of collecting, processing, and transporting them for other use (Kneese and Bower 1979: 6). The production of hazardous wastes constitutes a negative externality because the costs of generation are not fully internalized in the costs of producing the goods or services that result in hazardous waste by-products.

A second rule of thumb sanctions intervention when externalities affect public goods (Stone 1982: 98). Public goods are nondivisible resources to which access cannot readily be restricted. The externality costs associated with hazardous waste generation do, in fact, primarily affect public goods, including the following:

—air or water contamination due to improper disposal or handling
—resultant damage to public health
—resultant damage to wildlife, scenic values, and recreational resources
—costs to the public when governments incur expenses in remedial cleanup of abandoned hazardous waste treatment or disposal facilities or in providing health care or relocation assistance to affected individuals such as at Love Canal or Times Beach

Most economists who have analyzed environmental externalities have agreed that some form of intervention by government is justified (Freeman et al. 1973: 163–66). Much of the debate concerning governmental policy for managing environmental externalities has focused on the choice between market mechanisms and command-and-control regulation. In the arena of environmental quality policy, command-and-control regulation consists primarily of standards governing desired behavior and sanctions for violating those standards. Ideally, adherence to the standards should internalize the externality costs associated with such activities as hazardous waste generation. Sanctions should function both as an incentive for decision makers to adhere to the standards, and as an additional means of internalizing externalities (O'Brien 1978: 437).

The two major market mechanisms that have been promoted are constructing a property system in pollution rights (Aranson 1982; Coase 1960) and taxing externalities (Anderson et al. 1977; Baumol 1972; Levin 1982). Other alternatives that have been proposed to command-and-control regulation include restructuring liability and using subsidies. Each of these is examined in the following sections in the context of hazardous waste management.

Pollution Property Rights

The concept of property rights relies on the marketplace to achieve efficient allocations of goods for which alienable property rights can be established and where values for competing uses can be assigned. To apply this market mechanism to internalize externalities, government must be able to assign property rights to identifiable units of a given environmental amenity, such as air or water quality or environmental health. Individuals with competing interests in the use of the environmental amenity must be able to place a value on it. If these two conditions hold, and government establishes rules for the buying and selling of the units of environmental quality, the market should permit the achievement of efficient allocations. For example, when an industry that wishes to discharge pollutants to the air is willing to pay a price that equals the value placed on clean air by all individuals whose air quality property rights would be affected, the industry could buy those rights and proceed to discharge its effluent.

The nonexclusivity of the benefits of clean air and water and public health significantly constrain the use of a pollution property rights system (Cook 1988: 24). These constraints apply to hazardous waste management as well. The high transaction costs involved in buying and selling such rights from all affected individuals also present a significant constraint (Aranson 1982: 359–60; Stone 1982: 111–12, 115). Significant gaps in scientific understanding of the environmental and public health impacts of releases and exposure to individual hazardous wastes and combinations of wastes impose further constraints on the use of pollution property rights (Grisham 1986; Rodricks 1984; Smith 1987). These gaps in knowledge must be filled to estimate the full externality costs of hazardous waste generation.

Taxing Externalities

The purest form of taxing environmental externalities involves the imposition of emissions taxes or effluent fees on specific pollutants. Tax rates are based on the receptors' willingness to pay to avoid the pollution. This defines a level of pollution that is socially optimal (Stone 1982: 104–6) and internalizes the costs of the undesirable amount of pollution (Anderson et al. 1977: 40).

Difficulty in measuring the public's willingness to pay for a given level of pollution control significantly impedes applying the tax emission concept. A practical compromise has been suggested, however: government defines ambient standards for specified environmental media and uses the emissions tax as an incentive to obtain sufficient reductions in pollutant discharges (Baumol 1972).

Emissions taxes are regarded as inappropriate as the principal means of environmental quality control for toxic and hazardous substances. Determining the proper tax rate to achieve a given ambient environmental quality standard would be an imprecise process that would take considerable time and several adjustments by both government and industry. Detailed information on the marginal cost curves of individual industries for each substance of concern within a given geographic area would be needed to develop a first-order tax rate estimate. In addition, detailed scientific knowledge of the physical, chemical, and biological behavior of each substance within a specified ecological system would be required. The high level of potentially harmful impact from small quantities of toxic and hazardous substances argues strongly against using such an imprecise system of emissions control (Anderson et al. 1977: 41).

Restructuring Liability

The use of liability through private lawsuits as a deterrent to behavior that causes externalities is the strategy that minimizes intervention in the marketplace (Bardach and Kagan 1982). Efficiency and equity are achieved through reliance on the common law nuisance doctrine and operation of the private legal system. Government merely defines and administers the rules of procedure, including property rights and the legal process by which an individual who is harmed can seek compensation for an externality caused by another person. This approach has several deficiencies, however (Freeman et al. 1973: 163–66):

—litigation is a win/lose process that usually does not produce balanced or economically efficient results for the adversarial parties;
—high transaction costs and the free-rider problem may discourage harmed individuals from initiating a suit, especially when a public good is affected; and
—reliance on rules of proof of legal causation presents significant obstacles in many instances of environmental externalities when causal factors may be poorly understood, complex, and synergistic, and when there may be considerable lag time between causative actions and resultant effects.

Government manipulation of the legal process to counter some of these deficiencies has been proposed (Bardach and Kagan 1982: 265). Suggested changes include shifting the burden of proof from the plaintiff to the defendant and providing technical assistance to plaintiffs in developing and proving claims. One alteration in the burden of proof that has been suggested as an alternative to setting regulatory standards is applying strict liability to externalities (Marten 1981: 371).

As Rosemary O'Leary discusses in Chapter 4, strict liability has been imposed on hazardous waste generation, along with joint and several liability, in legal actions taken by government against generators whose wastes were treated or disposed of at abandoned hazardous waste facilities. This restructuring of liability has resulted from judicial interpretation of the federal Comprehensive Environmental Response, Compensation, and Liability Act (CERCLA), also known as the Superfund Act, and analogous statutes enacted by the states. Under strict liability, hazardous waste generators can be held liable for damages resulting from wastes they have produced, regardless of whether or not their actions have been negligent and regardless of the actions of second or third parties, such as waste transporters or the operators of treatment, storage, or disposal facilities. Under joint and several liability, a generator can be held financially liable for damages that exceed the proportion attributable to the generator's share of wastes disposed of at a site.

The effectiveness of imposing altered liability as an incentive for regulatory compliance will be limited by the imperfect information that regulated businesses have (Marten 1981: 371). Such an incentive will only work when business decision makers are aware of the potential consequences of their actions, the risks of those consequences, the precautions that should be taken, and how each precaution will affect the probability and cost of each possible consequence. The CERCLA liability system is not employed as a substitute for regulating hazardous waste management. It may operate, however, as a supplemental incentive for generators to manage their hazardous wastes in a manner that will reduce the risk of damage to public health and the environment.

Subsidies

Subsidies are frequently discussed as an alternative to regulation in the context of payments for positive externalities (Stone 1982: 104). Most discussion of subsidies in the realm of environmental quality management, however, has been in the context of creating incentives for industries to reduce negative externalities. These have included grants and loan subsidies and tax incentives for investments in capital equipment for pollution control, and unit subsidies for pollutant discharge reductions (Cook 1988: 22–23).

Economists have argued against using grants and loan subsidies or tax incentives on the grounds that they provide no incentive to polluters to discover and adopt more efficient process technologies (Bain 1973: 49) and few incentives to reduce or control the volume of residuals generated (Freeman et al. 1973: 146–47). Unit subsidies have been criticized because they may artificially maintain the profitability of firms that would be unprofitable if the full costs of externalities were internalized in the costs of production (Cook 1988: 22).

Subsidies may also include less direct forms of cost redistribution. Federal and state governments have sponsored and financed research and development and provided technical assistance to individual firms over the full range of environmental externalities (Hill et al. 1984; ICF Incorporated 1983; EPASBO 1984). From an economic standpoint, these programs subsidize the costs of acquiring and interpreting information needed to achieve regulatory compliance. Advocates of such subsidies argue, however, that such programs improve the ability of industries, especially smaller firms, to comply with regulations at a cost to the public that is less than that required to achieve compliance solely through inspections and sanctions.

Command-and-Control and the Compliance Problem

Strict reliance on regulation and a compliance system based on inspections and sanctions has been criticized as ineffective as well as inefficient. Drayton (1980:5) has argued that most environmental regulatory enforcement problems result from economic disincentives to compliance. When uncooperative polluters can delay compliance with "virtual impunity," voluntary compliance by other regulated firms is likely to be significantly reduced (Drayton 1980: 16, 18; Roberts and Bluhm 1981: 379). Enforcement can be hampered when the regulated population is large in number and has a high diversity of technologic processes subject to regulation. Voluntary compliance will also be constrained when regulated firms lack knowledge about the regulations or lack the technical expertise necessary to comply.

A high level of voluntary compliance is essential to a regulatory agency's effectiveness and the overall economic efficiency of government regulatory programs (Hawkins 1984: 122; Roberts and Bluhm 1981: 4–5; Scholz 1984b: 392). A drop from 95 to 90 percent compliance will at least double an enforcement agency's work load (Drayton 1980: 19). Voluntary compliance is especially needed in hazardous waste regulation, which includes an extensive national population of approximately 90,000 small quantity generators, 67,000 large generators, and 4,800 treatment, storage, and disposal facilities (Bozeman et al. 1986a: 55–56; Porter 1987: 2; Ruder et al. 1985: 1, 38).

Enforcement of hazardous waste regulations governing SQGs has been hampered by the large number of regulated firms and the difficulties in identifying which individual firms are subject to regulation. Keeping track of regulated SQGs is further constrained by the high rate of business starts and closures (Beers 1988). The large number of SQGs and their small contribution to the total volume of waste generated has generally resulted in a low priority for inspecting their facilities. Federal and state enforcement agencies have typically focused their inspection and enforcement efforts almost exclusively on large quantity generators.

A 1984 study of six states that regulated generators of less than 1,000 kg/mo concluded that most states intend to inspect SQGs about once every three years (Jones and Fax 1984a: 15). Actual enforcement actions against regulated SQGs were also found to be quite infrequent. In New Jersey it has been estimated that 10 to 15 percent of the regulated generators that are inspected annually qualify as SQGs (Jones and Fax 1984b: 69). Some inspection priority is also given to specific industries that are of particular concern. Enforcement priorities are based on imminent public danger. Therefore first priority is given to such cases as those involving spills, failure to use the manifest system, and illegal containment, transportation, and disposal practices (Jones and Fax 1984b: 70). About one out of eight enforcement cases per week involves a regulated SQG in New Jersey. One recent study concluded that at the national level individual SQGs are likely to be inspected only once every fifty years at current inspection rates (Finegan 1986: 68).

This section has provided a brief overview of the principal alternatives that have been proposed and employed for internalizing the externality costs associated with environmental residuals, especially those associated with the generation of hazardous waste. Given the consensus that pollution property rights and emissions taxes are not appropriate public strategies for contending with externality costs resulting from hazardous waste generation, the principal focus of the remainder of the book is on command-and-control regulation and the use of restructured liability and subsidies to facilitate compliance.

To complete the background needed to assess these policy alternatives, the following section reviews what is known about how decisions are made in small businesses. This assessment of decisionmaking theory and behavior serves as the foundation for a detailed examination in Chapter 3 of the factors that are thought to influence regulatory compliance behavior by individuals and organizations.

SMALL BUSINESS DECISIONMAKING

The behavioral model that underlies most public initiatives to internalize environmental externalities is based on the rational model of decisionmaking. The rational model is based on the behavior of individuals, and is extended to organizations on the assumption that they behave essentially as individuals. The bounded rationality model was developed primarily to explain organizational behavior, but it also reflects recognition of departures from the ideals of individual rational decisionmaking behavior. Most government intervention strategies reflect some elements of the bounded rationality concept of how organizations actually behave.

This section describes the rational model of individual and organizational decisionmaking, the behavioral economists' bounded rationality model, and their application to decisionmaking by small businesses.

Rational Decisionmaking

The rational model of decisionmaking holds that rational actors attempt to maximize their individual utility functions. They base their decisions on a comprehensive assessment of all the choice opportunities available and choose the action that will provide the maximum benefit or utility consistent with their goals and objectives. This model assumes that decision makers are knowledgeable of all the alternatives open to them, the consequences that each entails, and the present and future value of these consequences to them (Allison 1971: 31). It further assumes that the rational decision maker is able to compare the alternatives based on some common measure of utility (Allison 1971: 29–30; Cyert and March 1963: 44–45; Simon 1955: 99, 108, 110; Simon 1976: 61–78; Simon 1979: 500; Stover and Brown 1975: 363–75).

In the conventional theory of rational decisionmaking by business firms, it is assumed that the principal goal of decision makers is to maximize the value of the firm or its profits (Cooley and Edwards 1983: 27; Cyert et al. 1956: 237; Simon 1972: 162–63). Output and price decisions are assumed to be based on equating marginal cost and marginal revenue (Cyert and March 1963: 12).

Bounded Rationality

The bounded rationality model is based on the premise that real-world decision makers do not have the resources or computational capacity to be knowledgeable about all choices or their consequences and probabilities. It also assumes that most decision makers and organizations do not have an all-purpose utility function with which to evaluate diverse alternatives. The behavioral economists argue that decision makers within organizations or firms, even where they are owner-entrepreneurs, derive other utilities from the firm in addition to the financial rewards that result from profit maximization (Cyert and March 1963: 9; Simon 1959: 262). Thus policy interventions designed to effect desirable organizational behavior by influencing the marginal costs of production may not necessarily have the intended results.

Bounded rationality stresses the distinction between the decision maker's subjective environment, which he perceives, and his objective environment, that is, the "real" world (Simon 1959: 256). Thus the decision maker's actions cannot be predicted solely from facts about his objective world; information is also needed about what he perceives. The decision maker's perceptions reflect his training, experience, and goals (Cyert and March 1963: 120–22).

Bounded rationality assumes that rather than seeking optimal choices, decision makers "satisfice" by searching for satisfactory alternatives within the limits of their knowledge and computational resources (Cyert and March 1963: 113; Simon 1959: 262–64; Simon 1979: 501). The related theory of search suggests that new alternatives will be investigated only when none of the known alternatives is satisfactory, and that the search for alternatives will start in those areas that a firm views as being most under its control (Cyert et al. 1956: 237).

A threshold model of choice has been proposed that builds on the concepts of satisficing and problemistic search (Slovic et al. 1977: 242). The threshold theory suggests that individuals will not focus their attention on problems with perceived low probabilities of occurrence (Kunreuther 1982: 209). This concept has been applied to criminal deterrence theory and may be applicable to the compliance behavior of small businesses.

Behavioral economists argue that organizations do not behave as single rational actors or entrepreneurs (Allison 1971: 74; Cyert and March 1963: 10–11; Deeks 1976: 8; March and Shapira 1982: 97; McMillan 1980: 24; Roberts and Bluhm 1981: 15). The values and utility functions of equity owners in a firm may differ significantly from those of managers. Thus the assumption that decisionmaking within a firm is based on a single utility function is questioned (Allison 1971: 71–75; Simon 1955: 103–4; Simon 1976: 80–83; Simon 1979: 500–501). This suggests that the characteristics of individual decision makers and their positions within organizational decisionmaking systems may significantly affect decision outcomes in otherwise similar circumstances (Roberts and Bluhm 1981: 42–43).

Small-Business Decisionmaking Theory

Within small businesses, decisions on such matters as price, output, product mix, and internal resource allocation are frequently made by individual owner-entrepreneurs (Deeks 1976: 10). It has been suggested, therefore, that the traditional theory of the firm may be more applicable to small businesses. However, even in the realm of individual decision-making, conflicts in goals can be significant at any point in time, and utilities are subject to change over time (Einhorn and Hogarth 1982: 17–18). Thus the assumption of a single utility function probably does not apply to individuals any more than it does to organizations, and it is unlikely to apply to small businesses anymore than it does to large firms. However, within a small business decisionmaking is likely to be more centralized and, therefore, utility functions more nearly consistent over the short term (Kriesberg 1976: 111).

Individual Decisionmaking Studies

Experiments have been conducted to determine whether people actually employ utility functions in decisionmaking. In simple choice experiments, most subjects behave in a way consistent with the concept of maximizing utility, but when subjects are confronted with more complex, "real-life" decision situations, there is little evidence of behavior that results in utility maximization (Simon 1959: 258–59). Subjects also do not make substantive decisions that are consistent with what would be predicted by the rational model.

Recent insurance studies demonstrate the threshold concept. Individuals seem to have a strong preference for insuring against events characterized by high probabilities of occurrence, regardless of whether the resultant losses are great or small (Slovic et al. 1977: 243–45). For example, the perceived probability of flooding or earthquake has been found to define an important threshold in determining insurance purchases (Kunreuther 1982: 209). Individuals are not sufficiently concerned about a hazard to even contemplate purchasing insurance until the probability of the hazardous event occurring exceeds a particular level. However, this insurance action threshold varies among individuals.

The threshold model of choice appears to be driven by experience rather than an active search for information needed to assess attainment of an individual's action threshold. People in flood- or earthquake-prone areas have been found to have limited knowledge of the probabilities of the hazardous events occurring (Kunreuther 1976: 233–35). Homeowners who have experienced significant prior damage tend to rank the perceived severity of the potential hazard more highly than uninsured individuals (Kunreuther 1982: 209). They are also more likely to buy insurance (Kunreuther 1976: 248).

Organizational Decisionmaking Studies

There is no evidence from direct observation that firms actually equate marginal costs and revenues (Deeks 1976: 9; Simon 1979: 496). Numerous studies demonstrate that organizations satisfice rather than maximize utility (Cyert et al. 1956; Cyert and March 1963; March and Shapira 1982: 103; Simon 1959: 264). Businessmen's perceptions of problems have been found to be a function of their particular areas of expertise and personal experience (Dearborn and Simon 1958). A recent study of environmental management decisionmaking by utility companies demonstrates the influence of individuals' knowledge and experience on problem structuring and assessment of alternative choices (Roberts and Bluhm 1981: 339).

One of the more comprehensive studies of decisionmaking by small businesses was performed by Deeks (1976), who conducted onsite surveys of a stratified random sample of fifty small furniture companies in Great Britain with between twenty-five and seventy-five employees. Deeks found that owner-managers are emotionally and financially committed to their businesses to a degree quite different from salaried managers and administrators in larger firms. He concludes, however, that the rational model of profit maximization does not account for small business behavior. He notes that many small businesses pursue other goals at the expense of profits, such as specialization and craftsmanship, personal and family loyalties and, most often, survival rather than growth or profits. Small business goals may be highly specific to individual owner-managers and are likely to change with time as a function of development of the business and the socioeconomic circumstances of the owner.

Rice and Hamilton (1979) studied decisionmaking by 35 owner-managers of small businesses in Texas that ranged in size from 1 to 190 employees. They describe these managers as untrained in management and formal decisionmaking and overwhelmed with information that they can neither filter nor use. Most of the owner-managers based their decisions on "experience, intuition, and guesswork" rather than rational analysis of alternative choices.

Small-business owners or managers must fill multiple roles when they do not have the resources to hire management specialists (Dandridge and Sewall 1978: 28). They are forced to limit their analysis of individual problems and generally lack efficient means to screen information and identify optimal solutions to problems (Rice and Hamilton 1979: 7). Thus their own time constraints preclude attaining a thorough understanding of regulations and the technical means of complying with them (Steger et al. 1983: 2.33).

Small-business owners and managers typically have less technical expertise than their counterparts in larger firms. Deeks (1976) compared the educational backgrounds of managers of the small furniture companies he studied with those reported in several other studies of larger businesses in Great Britain (Acton Society Trust 1956; Clark 1966; Copeman 1955; National Economic Development Office 1965). He found that significantly smaller proportions of the smaller-business managers had attended British grammar schools (equivalent to secondary schools in the United States). Only one of the 229 smaller-business managers interviewed had graduated from a university. The differences were less pronounced for part-time continuing education courses: 59 percent of owners and 51 percent of managers in the small furniture firms versus 72 percent in Clark's study of larger businesses in the Manchester area. Deeks also found that very few of the small-business managers had received any formal management education.

Studies of management problems faced by small businesses have yielded similar lists (Deeks 1976: 139; Dandridge and Sewall 1978: 32; Peterson 1984: 41):

1. long-term business planning

2. keeping up-to-date with technical information

3. understanding legislation and regulations

4. paperwork and routine administration

5. such marketing techniques as pricing, advertising, and selling

6. financing, getting money, cash management

7. analyzing competition

Deeks (1976: 221) concludes that it is impossible for an owner-manager to be knowledgeable of all the management techniques required in his role as both entrepreneur and administrator.

Resource limitations are most frequently cited as the reason why small firms are unable to engage in the sophisticated strategic planning and decisionmaking processes prescribed for larger firms. These constraints include the following: lack of time and multiple demands on chief executives, limited financial resources, and lack of trained personnel (Cohn and Lindberg 1974: 4, 45; Shuman 1975: 87; Van Hoorn 1979: 85; Welsh and White 1981: 18). Most small firms must hire outside consultants to deal with specialized management problems or attempt to deal with such problems with less sophisticated internal techniques (Deeks 1976: 222).

IMPLICATIONS

The evidence concerning how decisions are made in small businesses suggest that government intervention strategies cannot rely exclusively on incentives and inducements targeted at the marginal costs of production. Many small businesses evidently base their decisions on utility functions other than firm profitability, and many decision makers apparently do not perform the equivalent of marginal analysis in weighing alternative courses of action. To the extent that small-business decision makers take account of costs and benefits, the government may need to actively influence decision makers' perceptions of the costs and benefits of alternative actions. Public policy makers may also have to contend with the existence of individual action thresholds keyed primarily to the probability of consequences rather than the magnitude of costs or benefits. Finally, policy makers and program administrators must anticipate that limited time available to small-business decision makers and limited expertise in technical matters pertinent to a given area of environmental management may significantly influence the response of small businesses to particular incentives and inducements. This is likely to be true whether public intervention involves changes in liability, command-and-control regulations, or subsidy programs.

3

Small Business Compliance

Command-and-control regulations that rely on sanctions and inspections for enforcement are based on a model of organizational compliance behavior that has its roots in the rational model of firm decisionmaking. As is the case for the decisionmaking models discussed in Chapter 2, the fundamental model of compliance behavior is a model of how individuals behave—the rational deterrence model. Studies of corporate compliance suggest, however, that additional variables must be considered to explain organizational compliance behavior; variables that reflect many of the assumptions of the bounded rationality model of decisionmaking.

This chapter completes the theoretical foundation for assessing governmental alternatives for influencing hazardous waste management by smaller generators. I begin by reviewing the rational deterrence model of compliance and examining the evidence for its applicability to both individual and organizational behavior. I then review concepts of corporate compliance behavior and assess the results of corporate compliance studies, including several recent studies of compliance with environmental regulations and compliance by small businesses. The chapter concludes with a discussion of the applicability of these models to understanding compliance behavior by small businesses.

SANCTIONS, DETERRENCE, AND RATIONAL COMPLIANCE

Environmental regulations typically prescribe what a business is to do and what the maximum civil and criminal penalties are for noncompliance.

For instance, hazardous waste generators are required to dispose of regulated hazardous wastes in permitted disposal facilities. The maximum civil penalty for failure to comply is a $25,000 per day fine (42 U.S.C. Section 6928(g)). Criminal penalties range as high as $50,000 per day with prison terms of two to five years (42 U.S.C. Section 6928(d)).

A firm that violates a regulation, for example, by disposing of wastes in an unlicensed landfill on its property, faces the possibility of being inspected by the state or federal environmental enforcement agency. If the inspector detects the violation and the enforcement agency initiates an enforcement proceeding, the noncompliant firm will incur the costs of defending itself and may be assessed the maximum fine or some lesser penalty. In addition, the firm will incur the costs of subsequently complying with the regulation. The firm may also realize other costs of noncompliance, such as a tarnished public image if the violation receives substantial publicity, or an antagonistic relationship with the enforcement agency that may extend to other regulatory areas.

The rational compliance model portrays compliance decisionmaking as a balancing of the costs and benefits of compliance versus noncompliance. A rational decision maker will compare all of the costs and benefits of compliance with the costs and benefits of noncompliance as the basis for deciding whether to comply with a given law or regulation (Ehrlich 1974: 69–72; Greer and Downey 1982: 490–91; Linder and McBride 1984: 338; Nagel 1974: 692–93; Stover and Brown 1975: 368–70; Viscusi and Zeckhauser 1979: 438, 445–46).

These costs and benefits can be classified as calculative or normative. Calculative variables involve the use of "an algorithmic or heuristic calculus" to evaluate specific decision factors, whereas normative variables "employ supraordinate value structures" or norms to evaluate compliance versus noncompliance (Greer and Downey 1982: 490). Norms "represent value judgments with respect to modes of behavior in social situations" (Miles 1980: 47).

Calculative Costs and Benefits

The calculative costs of compliance with prescriptive regulations, such as those governing hazardous waste management, consist of the opportunity costs of expending resources to perform the stipulated tasks, for example, using permitted disposal facilities, labeling containers, and training personnel. The calculative costs of noncompliance include the costs of being charged with a violation (legal defense costs, social stigma, public image damage); the costs of formal legal sanctions following conviction, such as fines or incarceration, and the costs of informal social and organizational sanctions (again social stigma, public image damage, etc.);

and the costs of subsequent compliance (DiMento 1986: 72; Diver 1980: 263, 266; Gibbs 1975: 64–66, 100; Greer and Downey 1982: 491–92; Nagel 1974: 699, 701–2; Stover and Brown 1975: 367; Tittle 1980: 9–10; Viscusi and Zeckhauser 1979: 441).

The calculative benefits of compliance consist mainly of avoiding the costs of noncompliance (Greer and Downey 1982: 492). The calculative benefits of noncompliance include benefits to the individual or organization from avoiding the costs of compliance with prescriptive laws or regulations (Greer and Downey 1982: 491–92; Viscusi and Zeckhauser 1979: 441).

Informal Sanctions

The informal sanction of social stigma may deter the average citizen more than the formal procedural and substantive punishments (Gibbs 1975: 84). Studies of individual compliance behavior indicate that the general public is more constrained by the threat of social stigma than the formal sanctions that attend criminal noncompliance. This suggests that people who are not habitual offenders seldom take formal legal sanctions into consideration in making behavioral decisions (Miller et al. 1971: 221; Tittle 1980: 321).

Two types of informal sanctions may be operative in corporate compliance decisionmaking: labeling as a "bad actor" by regulatory agencies and social stigma that may accompany publicity of alleged violations or enforcement actions. Hawkins (1984: 116) concludes from his study of the enforcement of water quality regulations in Great Britain that corporations avoid being labeled as uncooperative by enforcement personnel because public authorities will be more inclined "to lay blame for other problems at the door."

A number of authorities have suggested that social stigma has little effect on corporate compliance except when that stigma is likely to be attached to individuals within the organization rather than to the organization as a whole (Kadish 1963: 304). This is most often the case when the sanctions are criminal rather than civil (Braithwaite 1984: 319; Geis 1982: 53). On the other hand, there is considerable evidence that businesses strongly value their public image as a good in itself and that the threat of damage to the corporate image can be a strong deterrent (Braithwaite 1984: 319; Clinard and Yeager 1980: 30–1; Fisse and Braithwaite 1983: 229; Hawkins 1984: 8; Kadish 1963: 304).

Geis (1982: 63) found that corporations prosecuted in a heavy electrical equipment price-fixing case continued to make alibis in public even after the close of the case, which he suggests may imply that "loss of goodwill, more than loss of money or even an agent or two, might be the sanction feared most." Hawkins (1984: 116) quotes water quality enforcement officers in Great Britain who maintain that a firm's public image is protected as a good in itself.

Certainty, Severity, and Delay

The rational decision maker not only assesses costs and benefits, he or she also evaluates the certainty that these costs and benefits will accrue to him or her. This expectation factor is represented primarily by the decision maker's estimation of the probabilities of being apprehended and subsequently penalized and forced to comply. The concept of subsequent compliance includes a delay factor. In the case of prescriptive laws and regulations, rational decision makers would be expected to discount the costs of compliance based on their estimates of how long they can forestall having to make compliance expenditures.

The rational decision maker is assumed to weight the calculative costs of noncompliance based on these certainty and delay variables (Becker 1974: 9–10; Linder and McBride 1984: 338; Polinsky and Shavell 1979: 882; Stigler 1970: 527; Viscusi and Zeckhauser 1979: 442, 445). A number of authors have suggested, however, that decision makers do not explicitly calculate the product of certainty and severity (Tittle 1980: 210). It is argued that instead decision makers consider certainty and severity independently as additive variables.

Most studies of individual deterrence have shown a positive correlation between sanction certainty and compliance, but few have demonstrated a significant relationship between sanction severity and compliance (Jacob 1980: 71; Nagin 1978: 96; Tittle 1980: 7–8). It has been argued that sanction certainty should have a greater effect on organizational compliance behavior than sanction severity because it affects both the expected direct penalty for compliance and the expected subsequent incurring of the direct costs of compliance (Linder and McBride 1984: 344).

The severity of financial sanctions may be a more significant factor in corporate versus individual compliance decisions, however, if one assumes that the goal of profit maximization drives corporate decisionmaking (Anonymous 1979: 1235–36; Braithwaite 1984: 331; Kramer 1982: 81; Kriesberg 1976: 1107; Lane 1966: 90; NTSB 1979: 13). This assumption has not been empirically tested (Braithwaite 1984: 331; Geis 1982: 304). Nevertheless several authors argue that most fines are not high enough to have a deterrent effect (Braithwaite 1984: 331; Kovel 1969: 154). DiMento (1986: 51) cites recent penalties leveled under California's clean air regulations as an example. He notes that in one reporting period, the total amount of fines paid by forty-five industrial violators was less than $15,000 and the maximum individual fine was $800.

Normative Costs and Benefits

The normative costs of compliance assumed to be considered in the rational decision maker's calculus consist of conflicts with organizational and individual values and norms that are violated by regulatory requirements. For example, some business people strongly believe that certain decisions are outside the legitimate purview of government regulation (Greer and Downey 1982: 491; Jacob 1980: 71; Kadish 1963: 306; Krislov 1972: 339; Lane 1966: 94–95; Packer 1968: 359; Sabatier and Mazmanian 1981: 22). Others may view a particular law or regulation as unfair (AICPA 1983: 23–24; DiMento 1986: 72, 88; Hawkins 1984; Witte and Woodbury 1983: 137).

Scholz (1984b: 400) hypothesizes that corporate decision makers' attitudes toward the legitimacy of laws and enforcement activities probably play some role in compliance behavior, especially when "a firm's self-interest is not easy to perceive." Newman (1958: 60) suggests that some cases of corporate crime may constitute a conscious protest of what corporate decision makers consider to be illegitimate government infringements on business. Sanctions may be more effective when laws are generally viewed as fair and legitimate, since people who are willing to violate such laws may be motivated to a greater extent by the opportunity for personal gain (Tittle 1980: 177). The potential threat of social stigma may be ineffectual when the legitimacy of a law or regulation is questioned within the corporate culture (Kadish 1963: 305).

A study of self-reported compliance with several laws found that individuals who felt that speeding and marijuana laws were "right" were more likely to comply with them (Jacob 1980: 78). A second study of self-reported deviant behavior by individuals yielded statistically significant correlations (alpha level of 0.05 or better) between compliance behavior and individuals' ratings of how "morally wrong" different deviant acts were (Tittle 1980: 171, 175–76). In a review of the income tax compliance literature, Witte and Woodbury (1983: 137) conclude that compliance is more likely among those who perceive their individual tax status as equitable.

The normative costs of noncompliance derive from conflicts with organizational and individual norms that dictate compliance, for example, a high value placed on obeying laws *per se* (Becker 1974: 10; Greer and Downey 1982: 491–92; Stover and Brown 1975: 367). The normative benefits of compliance and noncompliance involve adhering to the organizational and individual norms that respectively support or constrain compliance (Greer and Downey 1982: 491–92).

There is little empirical evidence to support significance of normative noncompliance cost variables, with the exception of one study of prospective compliance with Occupational Safety and Health Act (OSHA) regulations by management and production executives. In that experiment, individuals who scored higher on measures of personal law-abidingness were also more likely to project compliant behavior in the regulatory context tested (Greer and Downey 1982: 495). However, in ten similar experimental settings, normative noncompliance variables were not significantly correlated with prospective compliance behavior.

Much of the observed variation in individual compliance behavior remains unexplained, even when more comprehensive, causal analytic models have been employed. All of the quantitative studies of deterrence theory have moderately low to low R^2 values for regression models of compliance behavior. These range from 0.37 to 0.40 for some of the more comprehensive models (Jacob 1980) and as low as 0.02 to 0.12 for more restricted models (Clinard et al. 1979; Grasmick and Appleton 1977). Thus there is evidence to suggest that other factors must also be considered to explain compliance behavior beyond the calculative and normative rational cost and benefit variables.

BOUNDED RATIONALITY AND CORPORATE COMPLIANCE

Corporate compliance theory is built on the rational deterrence theory and is supplemented with concepts derived from the distinction between individual and organizational decisionmaking (Anonymous 1979: 1365; Braithwaite 1984; Clinard and Yeager 1980; Geis 1967; Kramer 1982; Scholz 1984b; Sutherland 1949).

Narrowly applied, the rational compliance model includes the assumptions of comprehensive knowledge of alternatives, consequences, and probabilities, and employment of a unitary utility function. There is considerable evidence, however, that limited information, subjective perception, and multiple conflicting values result in both individual and organizational compliance behavior that can significantly deviate from what would be expected of the strictly rational decision maker.

Reality Versus Perception

The distinction between actual and perceived decisionmaking variables is one of the most important qualifications that must be made in modifying the rational compliance model to explain real world behavior (Diver 1980: 266; Gibbs 1975: 100, 115, 118–19; Simon 1959). Empirical studies that attempt to explain compliance behavior based on statutory sanction levels and actual probabilities of apprehension and enforcement are less likely to predict observed behavior than those that measure decision makers' perceptions of these variables.

Salience, Knowledge, and Clarity

Recognition of the importance of the difference between the objective world and people's perceptions of it emphasizes the importance of knowledge limitations to understanding compliance behavior. It is likely that in many instances, corporate noncompliance legitimately results from lack of knowledge of the applicable regulations (DiMento 1986: 104; Lane 1966: 96). Corporations may also have difficulty estimating the costs of alternative responses to regulations. Roberts and Bluhm (1981: 27) found this to be the case even with the large electric utilities they studied.

The complexity of rational compliance calculations is illustrated by a formula used by the federal EPA to determine penalties based on estimated noncompliance benefits (Diver 1980: 265). The formula uses fifteen financial parameters in twenty-seven steps, and results are very sensitive to several highly uncertain predicted values, such as future inflation rates, useful life of pollution control equipment, and return on equity.

Corporations have enhanced their ability to deal with complex regulatory environments, such as those posed by environmental and health and safety regulations, by establishing in-house units of experts specializing in such areas as environmental protection. Nevertheless, in a survey of corporate environmental protection experts, the majority interviewed said that keeping current with regulations occupied most of their time and that they were unable to devote enough time to monitoring internal and external environments "in search of uncontrolled problems" (Scholz 1984a: 147).

Not only are limited knowledge and expertise constraints on compliance; the lack of clarity in the laws and regulations can pose a substantial barrier to rational compliance decisionmaking. Environmental laws often pose considerable problems to firms that attempt to understand and apply them to specific situations. Difficulties include extremely complex definitions, unspecified compliance deadlines and standards, and inconsistencies between statutes and regulations (DiMento 1986: 104). It has been suggested that a dedicated staff of lawyers is needed to interpret environmental laws when firms seek to fully comply (DiMento 1986: 104, 187).

Firms are not likely to take the initiative when positive action is required by a regulation until the costs of compliance and noncompliance are made more clear, for example when they are confronted by a regulatory agency with a demand for specific action and the alternative of a specific sanction (Roberts and Bluhm 1981: 27; Scholz 1984a: 146). In-house compliance expertise may enhance a firm's ability to make rational compliance decisions but may not necessarily result in enhanced compliance from the perspective of the regulatory agency. DiMento (1986: 104) notes that "lawyers are trained to react to law in ways that do not always favor compliance." A number of large firms have dedicated compliance staffs who view compliance in "narrow, sometimes counterproductive and begrudging ways" (DiMento 1986: 187).

Sanction Certainty and Severity Thresholds

Several authors have speculated that deterrence operates at a threshold level in compliance decisionmaking by individuals, rather than as a continuous function (Jacob 1980: 70; Tittle 1980: 8). Deterrence may not occur until the threat of sanction (a function of both severity and certainty) is sufficiently high. The relationship beyond that threshold may be linear, curvilinear, or even step-wise with multiple threshold points.

The concept of sanction severity and certainty thresholds is similar to the probability thresholds that have been identified in modeling insurance purchase behavior for the low-probability events discussed in Chapter 2 (Kunreuther 1976; 1982; Slovic et al. 1977). Tittle (1980: 236, 322) found evidence of threshold effects in individual compliance behavior for several sanction characteristics. Deterrent effects were only associated with high levels of certainty for informal sanctions and high levels of severity for formal sanctions. Mid-level thresholds were found for severity of informal sanctions and certainty of formal sanctions with continuously increasing deterrent effects above the thresholds.

Organizational Variables

Because business firms are collections of individuals, compliance behavior can be expected to differ from that predicted by the rational model for individuals. Variables that are likely to have a significant effect on corporate compliance behavior include the following: financial condition, organizational structure and size, organizational goals, the external environment of the organization, and organizational culture. Each of these is discussed briefly in the following sections.

Firm Financial Condition

Several studies have documented a relationship between poor financial condition of firms and greater involvement in antitrust violations (Clinard et al. 1979: 151). Other studies have demonstrated an association between firm profitability and decreased likelihood of violating trade practice laws and labor statutes (Lane 1966: 92–95).

Clinard et al. (1979: 156–58, 163) compared total numbers of violations and violations of manufacturing, environmental, and labor laws for the 477 largest Fortune 500 corporations during 1975 and 1976 with ten measures of financial health based on three financial performance concepts: profitability (net income divided by total firm assets), efficiency (total sales divided by total assets), and liquidity (a firm's working capital—difference between current assets and current liabilities—divided by total assets).

They found that fourteen of eighteen significant standardized regression coefficients were negative, indicating higher violation rates per unit size for firms in poorer financial health. They also report that ten of eleven significant coefficients were negative for five-year trend measures of profitability, efficiency, and liquidity. While the financial condition variables were found to be significantly correlated to compliance behavior, they did not explain a large amount of the observed variance in behavior. The individual standardized regression coefficients for these variables were quite small, ranging from 0.09 to 0.29, and the R^2 values for equations based only on financial performance were also low, ranging from 0.02 to 0.05 (Clinard et al. 1979: 164–65).

Clinard et al. (1979: 150, 166–67) suggest that different variables may control corporate compliance behavior in different regulatory contexts. They found considerably different relationships between firm and industry financial performance measures and violation rates for four different classes of regulations: administrative, environmental, manufacturing, and labor.

There may be a need as well to differentiate between proscriptive and prescriptive laws. Proscriptive laws are more likely to constrain illegal profit making while prescriptive laws are more likely to require firms to take actions that will cost them money. Firms that are in financial distress may be more likely than profitable firms to violate such prescriptive laws as environmental and health and safety laws since these would represent further drains on already strained resources.

Organizational Structure and Size

There are conflicting theories as to the effects of organizational structure on corporate compliance behavior. Individuals within large organizations allegedly feel less responsibility for the effects of their actions on society. "[E]ach individual is part of a whole that no one of them fully admits. No individual has done anything heinous, but the collective fault is unquestionable. . . . " (Braithwaite 1984: 326).

Clinard and Yeager (1980: 44–45) maintain that "size, delegation, and specialization . . . combine to produce an organizational climate that allows abdication of a degree of personal responsibility for almost every type of decision." They present one view that rigid hierarchical organizational structures can lead to the interpretation of organizational goals, such as production or product development goals, as absolutes that may justify any means to their achievement. They suggest, however, that the more likely process is the evolution of tacit understandings whereby upper management does not inquire about the details of how goals are being met and lower-level management and line employees do not tell them. Clinard and Yeager also submit that high degrees of specialization and delegation can lead to collective results that may be illegal without the awareness of individual decision makers.

Kramer (1982: 85) suggests that the organizational structure of Ford Motor Company translated the overall goal of profit maximization into subgoals that were linked with Ford's failure to modify the Pinto for safety reasons. He alleges that subgoals that required the car to weigh less than 2,000 pounds and cost less than $2,000 defined the task environment that led to rejection of the needed safety modifications.

The organizational structure of a firm may serve to preserve and support corporate culture and norms (Kramer 1982: 85; Sutherland 1949). But several studies suggest that the attitude of upper management, especially the chief executive officer, establishes the organizational norms with respect to corporate compliance (Braithwaite 1984: 322; Clinard and Yeager 1980: 60).

Organizational structure is related to organizational size. Larger firms are likely to have more complex and impersonal decisionmaking structures. Thus these phenomena may be more pertinent to large firms than small firms. But other relationships make the probable association between firm size and compliance behavior less straightforward.

Larger firms may be more likely to violate laws because they will be less severely affected by typical fines and can afford better legal counsel (Clinard et al. 1979: 154). On the other hand, at some size threshold, lack of technical and legal expertise may result in greater levels of noncompliance due to inadvertent violations. Smaller firms may be more severely impacted by adverse publicity resulting from an enforcement proceeding, since they "have less flexibility and power to evade the consequences of a publicity onslaught" (Fisse and Braithwaite 1983: 237). Yet smaller firms may be less subject to public scrutiny in the first place, since they are likely to be less visible, and they may be less concerned about public image. However, small firms that sell their products directly to the public may be even more susceptible to damage from adverse publicity, particularly when it involves product quality or consumer fraud. Others suggest that larger firms are more likely to be concerned for their reputations, whereas smaller businesses are more likely to be "motivated solely by profit" (Hawkins 1984: 114).

Organizational Goals

As previously noted, it has been suggested that corporate crimes are more subject to deterrence because it is assumed that they are motivated primarily by economics. Several authors have pointed out, however, that organizations do not typically have unitary utility functions or centralized decisionmaking processes (Braithwaite 1984: 331; Clinard and Yeager 1980: 47). They suggest that while much corporate crime does, in fact, reflect the pursuit of corporate profit, other goals may also come into play. Braithwaite (1984: 331) argues that a decision to compromise a product quality standard might not necessarily be done with the intent of increasing profits. It might be done "to foster the growth of a corporate subunit, or to protect the scientific standing of a new discovery."

External Organizational Environment

An organization's external environment encompasses not only the physical community in which it is situated, but the environment of the industrial sector of which it is a part. This includes trade associations, the markets in which a business operates, and the government agencies with which it interacts.

Economic and legal conditions have been identified as two of the most significant external environmental factors pertinent to corporate crime. Kramer (1982: 88) suggests that the impact of external environmental conditions on the attainment of organizational goals may help explain corporate deviance. He suggests that in the Pinto case, competition from foreign automakers motivated Ford to rush the production of the Pinto. Geis (1967: 130–31) observes that the uncertainty posed by competition may be one of the bases for collusion and price fixing. He reports that in the heavy equipment price-fixing conspiracy of the 1950s, price-fixing arrangements ebbed and flowed in response to market conditions and the level of enforcement activity.

Leonard and Weber (1970: 136–37, 146) and Clinard and Yeager (1980: 52) argue that significant market power, due to high market concentration, entry barriers, economies of scale, and product differentiation can create conditions that may induce illegal activity. Leonard and Weber cite the automobile dealership franchise system, which they say pressures dealers to sell cars at low margins, demotes service to a "necessary evil," and induces dealers to recoup low sales margins through deceptive and fraudulent practices that generate higher margins on used car sales and repairs.

Contradictory findings have been generated from studies of the relationship between market structure and corporate antitrust violations. Some show a positive correlation between market concentration and antitrust violations; others show a negative correlation; and one found no significant relationship (Clinard et al. 1979: 152). In their study of large corporate violations, Clinard and Yeager (1980: 131) did not find evidence of greater violations per unit size for firms with greater market power.

It has been suggested that in highly competitive industries firms may "engage in such violations as false advertising and bribery to sell products" (Clinard and Yeager 1980: 52). It has also been observed that smaller businesses typically operate in highly competitive markets and therefore have additional incentives to avoid the costs imposed by prescriptive environmental and health and safety regulations (Deyle 1985: 32).

Organizational Culture

Organizational culture is "the body of customary beliefs and social forms within an organization" (Miles 1980: 47). Some of the manifestations of corporate culture include "a company's reward structure, its propensity for risk taking, its attitudes toward growth, its emphasis on product or process, and the extent of its assignment of responsibility for company actions to formal groups" (DiMento 1986: 160).

Sutherland (1949), in his theory of differential association, stressed the role of learned goals and values from association with like-minded individuals within an isolated corporate environment as one of the factors that leads to corporate crime. Clinard and Yeager (1980: 58, 60–61) suggest that the norms that affect corporate decisionmaking are a function of both internal organizational culture and the norms of the industry within which a firm operates: "[a] corporation may socialize its members to normative systems conducive to criminality."

Geis (1967: 129) finds support for Sutherland's differential association hypothesis in his study of the heavy electrical equipment antitrust cases of 1961. He also found evidence that supports the role of national trade conventions as sites for corporate criminal conspiracies. Lane (1966: 101) also claims to have found evidence of differential association. He reports that in some shoe manufacturing communities almost half of the firms were charged with violating labor relations laws, while in others no firms were charged. Clinard and Yeager (1980: 299) found evidence in their study of the largest Fortune 500 corporations of more violations in certain industries, which they attribute to "industry culture." Nevertheless, correlations between industry type and violation rate could reflect other industry-specific variables that are a function of process characteristics (for example greater OSHA or environmental violations), or labor intensity (labor relations violations), or agency enforcement priorities.

Clinard and Yeager (1980: 299) conclude that one of the main factors that differentiates firms that frequently violate laws from those that do not is the corporate culture or "ethical climate." Kramer (1982: 85) cites the case of the Ford Motor Company's failure to modify the Pinto, despite recognition of the hazards it presented, as evidence of the role of corporate norms. He reports that "safety was not a strongly held norm at Ford, that it was not a part of the role prescription of Ford engineers or executives, and that concern for safety was negatively sanctioned."

Organizational Compliance Studies

Very few empirical studies of organizational compliance have been conducted. This section reviews the results of a series of studies of prospective compliance by individuals in hypothetical organizational settings, several studies of corporate compliance with environmental regulations, and studies of compliance by small businesses.

Prospective Compliance

Greer and Downey (1982) present a summary of empirical research on prospective regulatory compliance by individuals in organizational contexts based on their Compliance with Social Legislation (CSL) model. All of the studies employed a projective technique with which student or corporate executives or managers evaluate a scenario in which a manager violates a specific social regulation. Five questions are asked to measure each of eight independent variables categorized as driving forces (assumed to promote compliance) or restraining forces (assumed to constrain compliance):

1. organizational calculative driving forces
2. organizational calculative restraining forces
3. organizational normative driving forces
4. organizational normative restraining forces
5. individual calculative driving forces
6. individual calculative restraining forces
7. individual normative driving forces
8. individual normative restraining forces

Eight student test groups and three groups of managers or executives were used with noncompliance scenarios that included regulatory requirements promulgated by the OSHA, water pollution control regulations from the EPA, and other regulations enforced by the Federal Trade Commission (FTC), the National Labor Relations Board, and the Equal Employment Opportunity Commission, as well as federal tax regulations.

Organizational calculative restraining forces (costs of compliance to an organization) were negatively correlated with projected compliant behavior for all three management test groups and one student test group. The other significant variable categories for the management test groups were all different. For one group of managing and production executives with an OSHA compliance scenario, there was a positive correlation with individual normative driving forces (law-abidingness). For a group of wastewater treatment plant supervisors with the EPA water pollution control regulatory scenario, there was a significant positive correlation with organizational calculative driving forces (avoidance of fines, favorable public image, good customer or employee relations). For the third group, which involved executive vice-presidents and the violation of FTC regulations, there was a significant negative correlation with individual normative restraining forces (questioned legitimacy of the regulation). The patterns of significant variables for student subjects tested with the same noncompliance scenarios were different.

Greer and Downey (1982: 496) conclude that the salience of different decisionmaking variables differs with the regulatory context and with the type of decision maker. In the context of deterrence and corporate compliance theory, it is interesting to note that the calculative costs of noncompliance (organizational calculative driving forces), for example, sanctions, were only significant for one of the three management test groups and only one of eight student test groups.

Environmental Regulatory Compliance

Environmental regulatory programs typically require significant capital expenditures for technologically complex pollution control equipment and compliance with fairly complex performance standards and monitoring and reporting requirements. The major themes that emerge from studies of compliance with environmental regulations include problems of understanding the regulations, economic disincentives to compliance, and the need for strong enforcement programs that give the impression of high probabilities of apprehension and success by enforcement agencies in forcing compliance.

From 1970 through 1971, Marcus (1980) analyzed compliance with federal clean air regulations nationally and in Allegheny County, Pennsylvania (Pittsburgh). He found that small emitters (less than 100 tons of particulates and sulfur dioxide) and large emitters (more than 7,000 tons) tended to escape effective regulatory control, while firms in the middle range were primarily in compliance.

Marcus (1980: 216–20) interviewed various federal and state technical and legal officials and experts to assess the reasons for this binodal noncompliance pattern. Based on those interviews, he attributes the noncompliance of small emitters to decisions by enforcement agencies to not pursue enforcement with smaller sources. He attributes noncompliance by the larger sources, which were concentrated nationally in the nonferrous smelting, electric utility, and steel industries, to a combination of calculative and normative factors: high labor, raw material, and energy costs; foreign competition; capital shortages; pollution control technology problems; and questioned legitimacy of the air pollution regulations. He also identifies a number of normative and calculative factors as contributing to compliance, including personal norms, concern for community norms, and economic opportunity-taking, including the use of pollution reduction requirements to recycle salable or usable materials, save energy, or gain market share at the expense of competitors. Interview subjects suggested that the moderate-sized sources tended to comply in part because they lacked the technical and legal expertise to effectively fight the regulations.

Marcus clearly considers agency enforcement, through inspections and prosecutions, to be critical to achieving compliance. Drayton (1980: 18) also emphasizes the importance of environmental regulatory enforcement programs that give regulatees the impression that violations will be promptly detected and prosecuted. He reports that following the institution of a fine for late air quality monitoring reports by the Connecticut Commission for Environmental Quality, timely filings increased from 83 percent to 98 percent (Drayton 1980: 25).

Marten (1981), in his assessment of compliance with federal Department of Transportation (DOT) regulations governing hazardous materials transport, also attributes lack of compliance to inadequate agency enforcement. As evidence of the lack of voluntary compliance with those regulations, he cites the results of a DOT roadside inspection in 1979 when 291 violations were recorded from inspecting 297 vehicles, 16 of which were taken out of service because of the severity of violations (Marten 1981: 366).

The National Transportation Safety Board (1979: 3–6, 7–11), in a study of noncompliance with regulations governing the transportation of hazardous materials, surveyed officials in 11 federal regulatory agencies and 100 persons employed in the transportation industry. Government agency respondents identified six factors as contributing to noncompliance:

1. lack of awareness of the regulations
2. lack of understanding of the regulations

3. inability to stay current with the regulations because of their complexity

4. economic incentives (cost savings)

5. lack of adequate agency inspection and enforcement

6. inadequate training of personnel handling the materials

Industry respondents identified seven reasons:

1. technical difficulty of regulations and lack of expertise to understand them

2. lack of employee training

3. cost of employing adequately trained personnel to implement the regulations

4. perceived low risk of apprehension for violations

5. economic incentives to avoid drains on profits

6. lack of awareness of the regulations

7. resistance to change in procedures and processes

Roberts and Bluhm (1981: 323–34, 380, 384), in their study of environmental regulatory compliance by electric utility companies, observe that the lack of penalties for first offenders offers little incentive for firms to comply prior to being apprehended and forced to do so. On the other hand, they note that some utilities have instituted environmental controls that exceed regulatory requirements, apparently in an effort to forestall hostile action by environmentally sensitive interest groups in their host communities. Roberts and Bluhm also report that utility decision makers were less likely to voluntarily comply when they believed that regulations lacked scientific support or promised dubious social benefits, in other words, lacked legitimacy.

Small Business Compliance

It is often assumed that regulatory violations by small firms are the result of ignorance of the law and inadequate technical and legal advice. DiMento (1986: 156) summarizes the California South Coast Air Quality Management District profile of the most difficult firms to control as follows: "a combination of small size and concomitant lack of sophistication about the regulatory process."

Empirical studies of small business compliance have been few. Lane's (1966: 98–99) analysis of 1948 violations of the Fair Labor Standards Act and Public Contracts Act by firm size categories suggests some variation by industry group. His data show evidence of a binodal distribution of violations for two industry groups: textile and related products, and leather and leather goods, with peaks (42 percent of inspected firms in violation) in the 4–7 employees category (the smallest category) and secondary peaks in the 500 or more (35 percent) and the 200–499 (42 percent) employment categories, respectively. In the metals and metal products industry, he reports a monotonically declining violation rate with increasing size, ranging from 52 percent in the 4–7 employees size class to 22 percent in the 500 or more category.

Based on his investigation of a number of environmental compliance court cases, DiMento (1986: 21) concludes that many regulatory offenses by small businesses lack criminal intent and are more accurately characterized as inadvertent or negligent. He cites examples that include the following: "failure to secure one of several permits, to provide complete information, or to maintain control technology." Small businesses frequently do not realize the cost of noncompliance. DiMento (1986: 86) quotes one small businessman who said he would have gladly purchased the required environmental control equipment had he realized the cost he would incur defending himself in an enforcement lawsuit.

In a study of tax collection compliance by 250 small businesses in Washington State, Mueller (1963: 3) found "a general lack of knowledge on the part of the small businessman as to his tax responsibilities and liabilities." He concludes that the complexity of state and local tax structures is partly to blame, but he also suggests that to a greater extent lack of knowledge is the result of "unwillingness or reluctance to make an effort to become informed about tax matters."

Mueller also found that those small businessmen who turned to public bookkeepers or tax advisors did not necessarily improve their tax collecting compliance. He observes that many of the "experts" hired proved to be incompetent as a result of small businesses trying to find the cheapest consultants available or not knowing where to find competent assistance.

IMPLICATIONS FOR SMALL BUSINESS COMPLIANCE

The simpler organizational structure and greater centralization of decisionmaking in small businesses make it more likely that compliance actions will be the result of explicit decisions by individuals rather than emerging as the de facto consequence of a series of narrowly focused production decisions. Compliance actions are more likely to reflect the perceptions and attitudes of owners and upper-level managers, and there is likely to be greater individual accountability for compliance decisions. While it has been suggested that businesses may be more sensitive to the financial costs and benefits of compliance decisions than individuals, the evidence from the small-business decisionmaking literature presented in Chapter 2 suggests that many small-business owners do not base their decisions solely on a profit-maximizing basis.

The research literature on individual deterrence, as well as the more limited information on corporate compliance, suggests that small businesses may be responsive to the threat of formal sanctions for noncompliance. However, individual decision makers may have thresholds for both sanction severity and sanction certainty. It is likely that small-business decision makers will be more sensitive to sanctions with a higher certainty of enforcement than to those with a low perceived probability of imposition, even when formal penalties are relatively severe.

The threat of informal sanctions, including "bad actor" labeling by regulatory agencies and a tarnished public image, may affect the behavior of some small businesses. The limited information on informal sanctions indicates the effectiveness of this threat will vary with the personal attributes of decision makers in small businesses, the nature of the business's products or services, its public visibility, and the type of regulation. Social stigma costs are less likely to be evaded because of greater individual accountability for decisionmaking within smaller firms. Some small businesses may be especially vulnerable to public image damage because the nature of their business affords them high public visibility, for example dry cleaners or autobody shops. Others that do not produce products for direct public consumption, such as pesticide formulators and metal platers, may be largely insulated from public scrutiny.

Unfamiliarity with applicable laws and regulations is more likely to be a constraint on compliance by small businesses than larger firms because of the knowledge and time limitations faced by owner-entrepreneur decision makers. Small businesses are less likely to have access to the technical or legal expertise needed to stay abreast of and interpret complex regulations, such as those that pertain to environmental management. The financial condition of a small business may affect its willingness to make expenditures to comply with prescriptive regulations. This may be a greater constraint on small businesses that typically operate in more competitive markets.

There is only limited evidence that normative decisionmaking variables, such as perceived legitimacy of regulations and individual decision makers' personal values of law-abidingness, are likely to have an effect on compliance decisions by individuals. While the personal values of individual decision makers may not be amenable to manipulation by the public sector, it may be possible to bolster the perceived legitimacy of specific regulations through a well-directed education and public relations effort.

The influence of internal organizational culture on compliance actions is not well documented. It is likely, however, that in small businesses the perceptions and attitudes of owners and upper-level managers have a more pervasive influence on compliance decisionmaking. The impact of external organizational culture on compliance behavior is also relatively speculative. There is evidence that firms from the same industrial sector respond similarly to specific laws and regulations, but the reasons behind these patterns are not clear. They may reflect collective norms, but they may also reflect shared information and common financial, labor, and technical constraints on compliance.

Chapter 5 presents what is known about the influence of many of these factors on adherence by smaller generators to selected hazardous waste regulations. That analysis focuses principally on the calculative compliance variables and the characteristics of small-business organizations and decision makers that affect compliance behavior. The influence of altered liability on adherence to hazardous waste regulations is also examined in Chapter 5. Rosemary O'Leary's detailed analysis of the liability exposure of smaller generators is presented in Chapter 4 as background to assessing this dimension of the costs and benefits that may influence compliance decisions by small businesses.

4

Legal Liability of Smaller Generators of Hazardous Waste

Rosemary O'Leary

INTRODUCTION

According to one EPA study, an estimated 264 million metric tons of hazardous waste are generated annually, enough to "fill the New Orleans Superdome almost 1,500 times over" (Boraiko 1984; Westat, Inc. 1984). Despite the fact that smaller generators of hazardous waste contribute only a fraction of that amount, they face potential site clean-up liability costs of considerable magnitude based on a number of federal, state, and municipal laws. This chapter begins by discussing the liability exposure of small businesses that generate hazardous wastes. An in-depth examination of the EPA's "de minimis" settlement policy follows. Examples of actual de minimis settlements are then discussed. The chapter closes with an overview of the implications of potential liabilities and defenses for smaller generator waste management practices.

CASE IN POINT

Consider the case of one smaller generator of hazardous wastes, ACME Dry Cleaners (a fictitious entity). This small business generates an estimated 350 pounds of hazardous wastes every month in the form of perchlorethylene, otherwise known as perc, PCE, or tetrachloroethylene. The company's hazardous wastes consist of still residues from solvent distillation, spent filter cartridges, and cooked powder residue. The com-

pany stores its wastes onsite in 55 gallon drums until enough have ac-
cumulated to make removal cost-effective. The owners of the dry cleaning
business do not know where the wastes are taken or how they are actually
disposed. In fact, up until 1987, the drums had been disposed of at the
local landfill which has just been declared a federal Superfund site.[1]

SITE CLEANUP LIABILITY

The potential liability facing this smaller generator of hazardous wastes
is great. First, suit potentially can be brought against ACME by a number
of plaintiffs: the federal government, the state government, a local government, or an individual. Next, ACME can be sued in a variety of
capacities, including as a generator of hazardous wastes,[2] as an owner
or operator of a waste generating facility at the time of the disposal of
hazardous wastes,[3] or as an individual who arranged for the disposal
of the hazardous wastes.[4] Last, ACME can be sued under a number of
federal statutes, most importantly the Comprehensive Environmental
Response, Compensation and Liability Act (CERCLA or Superfund) and
the Resource Conservation and Recovery Act (RCRA). Suit can also be
brought under state law. Many municipalities also have local ordinances
governing the disposal of hazardous wastes.

CERCLA LIABILITY

Enacted in 1980, CERCLA established a "Superfund" to enable the
federal government to clean up abandoned hazardous waste disposal sites.
It expanded the class of private parties liable for such sites, including
site owners and operators, waste transporters, and generators. The act
also authorized the EPA to go to court to force the abatement of hazardous
waste pollution at Superfund sites that pose an "imminent and substantial" threat to public health or the environment.[5]

Courts have universally held that CERCLA imposes strict liability,[6]
meaning a generator (including a smaller generator like ACME) may be
subject to liability even if it has not departed in any way from the standard
of reasonable care and has not violated any environmental laws. Additionally, when injury is indivisible, that is, when it is not clear whose
wastes caused what damage,[7] liability is joint and several.[8] Joint and
several liability means that the government can proceed against any one
or a group of potentially liable parties for the total cost of the cleanup
for which each is jointly or individually liable. If such liability is established, traditionally the only remedy for the defendants has been to seek

contributions from other responsible parties, if they can be found, through legal action.

Compounding the issue is the fact that the government need not prove that a defendant's actions were the cause of the environmental threat or harm in question.[9] Courts have held that CERCLA requires no more proof than showing that a generator sent out hazardous wastes for disposal, that the wastes ended up at a site at which a release or threatened release of any hazardous substance necessitated response action, and that wastes of the type the generator disposed of are present at the site.

RCRA LIABILITY

RCRA regulates hazardous wastes from generation to disposal or "cradle to grave." There are several major sections of RCRA that are of particular importance to smaller generators of hazardous wastes. These concern onsite storage of hazardous wastes (42 U.S.C.A. 6922–6925), a manifest system for tracking hazardous wastes from generator to transporter to disposal facility (42 U.S.C.A. 6922–6923), and federal minimum standards for hazardous waste disposal, enforced through a permit system for disposal facilities (42 U.S.C.A. 6924–6925).[10]

Pursuant to RCRA, when presented with evidence that the past or present handling, storage, treatment, transportation, or disposal of any waste may present an "imminent and substantial endangerment," the EPA may bring suit against any person who has contributed to the situation. Possible defendants include past or present generators, transporters, and owners or operators of treatment, storage, or disposal facilities. In such a suit, the EPA may order a smaller generator to refrain from specific activities, may order such a generator to take specific actions as deemed necessary by the agency, or both. The EPA may also take appropriate administrative action (42 U.S.C. 6973 (a)). Any person who violates a court order under such circumstances may be subject to fines of up to $5,000 for each day that the violation or noncompliance continues (42 U.S.C.A. 6973(b)).

If convicted of violating any other applicable requirements of RCRA, a SQG may face civil penalties of up to $25,000 per day (42 U.S.C.A. 3008(g)). Criminal penalties can be as high as $50,000 per day with imprisonment of two to five years (42 U.S.C.A. 3008(d)(7)(A)). Upon a second criminal conviction, the fine and/or jail sentence is doubled (42 U.S.C.A. 3008(d)(7)(A)). Additionally, the act contains penalties for the offense of "knowing endangerment" for which penalties can range up to $250,000 and/or fifteen years in prison (42 U.S.C.A. 3008(e)). If the defendant is an organization, that organization may be subject to a fine of up to $1 million for "knowing endangerment" (42 U.S.C.A. 3008(e)).

State Statutes

State statutes can also be used to bring suit against smaller generators of hazardous waste. Today most states have enacted hazardous waste regulatory programs that parallel RCRA and sometimes CERCLA. By law, state RCRA statutes and regulations must be at least as stringent as those of the federal government. Many are more stringent. In addition, many states allow pollution lawsuits based on negligence, trespass, or nuisance laws, although such causes of action have been more commonly replaced by environmental statutes. Any or all of these laws have been used alone or in conjunction with other state and federal laws to bring suit against smaller generators of hazardous wastes.

DE MINIMIS SETTLEMENTS

The stories of real and threatened lawsuits against smaller generators are legendary. For example, in California, two dentists annually disposed of small amounts of mercury and other substances used in the process of filling teeth. Their local landfill was declared a Superfund site and they were one of the few immediately ascertainable potentially responsible parties sued by the federal government for the cost of site remediation. In New York, an operator of a car painting facility routinely disposed of paint wastes in a local dump that was later the target of government action. While the waste contributed by the operation was miniscule in comparison to the total volume of waste disposed of at the site, this small volume contributor (SVC) was found to be jointly and severally liable for cleanup costs.

Legal defense fees and other transaction costs, such as suing other potentially responsible parties at hazardous waste sites, often exceed the amount that SVCs expect to pay based on the quantity and toxicity of their wastes. In response to the growing outcry from small volume waste contributors, Congress amended CERCLA in 1986 to recognize the concept of the "de minimis" waste contributor (42 U.S.C.A. 9622 (g)). A de minimis waste contributor is defined as:

1. a potentially responsible party,
2. who satisfies the requirements for liability (42 U.S.C.A. 9607),
3. and who does not have a valid defense,[11]
4. but who has made only a minimal contribution (by amount and toxicity) in comparison to other hazardous substances at the site.[12]

The main concept behind de minimis settlements is to assess those who contributed a minimal amount of waste to a site for response work based on such factors as toxicity and amount of waste. In exchange, settling parties obtain a promise by the federal government not to sue for response costs incurred under CERCLA or RCRA. Settling parties are also protected from suits by other potentially responsible parties (PRPs) seeking contribution for clean-up costs already covered in the de minimis settlement.

From the EPA perspective, de minimis settlements offer a swift and efficient way for SVCs to pay a sum in proportion to their involvement at the site, allowing them to be dismissed from further negotiations and litigation. In addition, de minimis settlements make EPA negotiations and litigation more manageable by allowing the early elimination of SVCs that are potentially responsible parties. Third, such settlements may increase the amount of response costs recovered through voluntary settlement agreements with SVCs. Fourth, de minimis settlements should foster settlement with major waste contributors by allowing the early collection of funds, which will reduce the overall liabilities of the larger contributors.

Determining Who Is a De Minimis Waste Contributor

The EPA's implementation of de minimis law is multifaceted, complex, and potentially contradictory. For example, the agency defines de minimis standing on a site-specific basis. Therefore, a generator that disposed of identical quantities of identical wastes at two different sites may be determined to be a de minimis contributor at one but not the other. The EPA's official policy follows:

> To qualify as a de minimis generator... the PRP must have contributed an amount of hazardous substances which is minimal *in comparison to* the total amount at the facility. The PRP must also have contributed hazardous substances which are *not significantly more toxic and not of significantly greater hazard effect* than other hazardous substances at the facility.... [emphasis mine][13]

For example, if 250 PRPs all disposed of organic solvents, then those PRPs that had contributed a minimal amount in relation to the total amount at the site could be designated as de minimis contributors. The key is that the SVCs' wastes were not more toxic or otherwise more hazardous than other substances disposed of at the site. Contrasted with this, if an SVC at the same site disposed of a minimal amount of a highly toxic or seriously hazardous waste (as compared with other substances at the site), the SVC would probably not qualify for de minimis status. The key in the second example is the potentially high cost of remediating the site contamination resulting from the more hazardous waste of the second SVC. Thus a firm that qualifies as a SQG or conditionally exempt generator based on monthly hazardous waste generation rate will not necessarily qualify as a de minimis contributor.

Current EPA De Minimis Policy

The CERCLA, as amended, gives the EPA discretionary authority to enter into expedited settlements when "practicable and in the public interest" if the settlement "involves only a minor portion of the response costs at the facility concerned" (42 U.S.C.A. 9622(g)(1)). To this end, the EPA's policy is to "focus on achieving comprehensive settlements in which interested de minimis PRPs at a particular site are addressed in *one* settlement agreement" [emphasis mine].[14] The SVCs are encouraged to organize and to present a unified, multi-party settlement offer to the government. The EPA has developed a standardized agreement with which regional EPA offices have been encouraged to avoid lengthy settlement negotiations with de minimis parties.

In order to facilitate such action by SVCs, the EPA will attempt to gather and release as expeditiously as possible information about PRP waste contribution at the site in question (42 U.S.C.A. 9622 (e)(1)). The agency may negotiate separately with PRP steering committees representing substantial numbers of SVCs. Finally, the agency may also consult with non-de minimis parties concerning its negotiations with SVCs since the toxicity and volume criteria established to define de minimis parties at a site will also determine which are non-de minimis PRPs.

Timing

While the general goal of EPA settlements with de minimis parties is to allow SVCs to quickly resolve their liability and without the need for extensive negotiations with the government, there are several factors that will influence the timing of de minimis settlements:

1. *The amount of information available about PRPs and their waste contributions to the site in question.* As a general rule, the EPA frowns upon de minimis settlements concluded prior to completion of a PRP search (including a title search and financial assessments).

2. *The amount of information available about the costs of reme-diating site contamination.* Generally the EPA will consider a de minimis settlement with an expansive covenant not to sue or without reservations of rights for cost overruns and future re-sponse action only when the agency is able to reasonably estimate the total response costs associated with cleaning up the site in question. Official EPA policy states that such a level of confidence is usually possible only after completing a Remedial Investigation and Feasibility Study and a Record of Decision.

3. *The nature of specific settlement document language* including any covenants not to sue or paragraphs concerning the future reopening of negotiations with SVCs should additional infor-mation become available.

4. *The amount of money paid by the settling parties.*

5. *The volume and toxicity criteria* used by the EPA to define a de minimis party.

The EPA policy also states that although different approaches may be used at different sites, each approach should seek to promote voluntary settlement, minimize transaction costs for both the PRPs and the gov-ernment, address the "legitimate interests" of all parties at the site, and assure that the level of risk to the EPA is "acceptable." EPA regional offices have been encouraged to attempt settlement with SVCs only if there is a "reasonable" chance of success.

Terms of Settlement

The terms of a particular settlement with SVCs will depend on timing and the factors enumerated above. While "early" settlements, that is, settlements negotiated at the beginning of the EPA's investigatory pro-cess, are not prohibited, they are potentially more problematic than late settlements. Pursuant to current EPA policy, for example, when an early settlement is negotiated, certain settlement paragraphs, called "reopen-ers," which concern possible renegotiation pending the collection of ad-ditional facts, "should be more expansive, and/or the premiums should be substantial." (A premium is an additional payment over and above a payment based on an SVC's volumetric share.) The rationale behind such a policy is to give the EPA added protection against the risk that new information may be discovered about a settling party's waste contribution to the site. In addition, in such a circumstance, the EPA will normally use more conservative criteria to distinguish between de minimis and non-de minimis parties, setting the volume and toxicity thresholds at low levels, so that major parties are not treated as de minimis parties. Finally, in such a situation the EPA will take into account the increased level of uncertainty through higher premium payments and other safeguards.

"Practicable and in the Public Interest"

As noted above, whatever the volume and toxicity of de minimis parties, a potential settlement with SVCs must be determined by the EPA to be "practicable and in the public interest" (42 U.S.C.A. 9622 (g)(1)). The EPA has not defined what is meant by these terms. Rather, to date the EPA has offered two examples of situations in which it would most likely *not* be practicable and in the public interest to settle with SVCs. First, if every waste contributor at a particular site is determined to be a de minimis contributor, the EPA will most likely not allow a de minimis settlement. Second, if several major parties at a site are bankrupt, the EPA would be less likely to "cash out" smaller contributors before reaching a settlement with the other parties.

Amount of Payment

How much will a de minimis settlement cost an SVC that has achieved de minimis status? EPA policy states that in the typical de minimis settlement the cash offer submitted by the de minimis parties must be at least equal to their volumetric share of the total past and projected response costs at the site. Because the waste in question must be of minimal toxicity before a party can achieve de minimis status, the nature of the waste is usually not relevant in calculating de minimis parties' payments. The "volumetric share rule," however, may be adjusted based on other factors, including the ability of all parties to pay, litigative risks, public interest considerations, value of a present sum certain,[15] inequities and aggravating factors, preliminary allocation of responsibility, and the nature of the case remaining against other parties after settlement.[16]

In addition, if the de minimis parties are able to negotiate a covenant not to sue that does not include reopeners for cost overruns and future response action, the cost of the settlement will increase. Moreover, the greater the uncertainty concerning PRPs, waste volumes, and costs of remedial actions, the higher the price of the "cash out." In the event that major PRPs agree to totally clean up a site, de minimis parties may find themselves negotiating with the major PRPs, not the government, or may find their negotiated settlement monies being paid to the major PRPs.

Enforcement of Payment

If an SVC achieves de minimis status and then fails to make an agreed upon payment or fails to comply with any other condition of the settlement, that SVC is subject to enforcement action, including assessment of the CERCLA civil penalties discussed earlier in this chapter (42 U.S.C.A. 9609). In addition, some settlement documents include a provision that permits the agreement to be vacated in the event of noncompliance.

CASES

Although very few de minimis settlement agreements have come to fruition, there are three examples that help illuminate EPA policy and the rationale behind it.

Cannons Engineering Sites

The first major de minimis settlement under CERCLA was announced in February 1988 (EPA 1988c). That case involved four sites in Massachusetts and New Hampshire used by the Cannons Engineering Corporation for the disposal of hazardous wastes. Four hundred and seventy-six PRPs, including school systems, airlines, laundries, printers, and gas stations were identified by the EPA, and total clean-up costs were estimated at $52 million.

In this case, the EPA defined a de minimis contributor as one that was responsible for less than 1 percent of the waste volume at each of the four sites with which they were associated. Initially, 272 PRPs were able to achieve de minimis status and settled with the EPA for a total of $10,960,292. Five months later, twenty-one PRPs were added to the de minimis list and paid an additional $541,467 (EPA 1988e).

The amount owed by each de minimis party included a volumetric share of the government's response costs, past and future; a settlement premium of 60 percent of the party's volumetric share of the total response costs to compensate for the risks posed by settling before all costs were known; and a base settlement charge to reimburse the government for its transaction costs. In exchange for these settlement payments, the government agreed to covenant not to sue for further civil or administrative liabilities. The settlement was criticized by major waste contributors at the site as allowing too large a share of the liability to be settled for too small an amount too early in the process. The EPA estimated that approximately 20 percent of the total cost of cleanup would be raised by the de minimis settlement.

U.S. v. Rohm & Haas Co.

In a second case, *U.S. v. Rohm & Haas Co.* (D.C., N.J., 1988), the EPA identified and sued sixteen companies that had contributed wastes to a landfill in Mantua, New Jersey, that later became a Superfund site. Tests at the site revealed the presence of mercury, toluene, benzene, and ethylbenzene. The chemicals had entered the groundwater and migrated into three surrounding lakes. The EPA and the state of New Jersey spent $10 million to construct a slurry wall around sixteen acres of contaminated soil and groundwater and to place a cap over the area.

Ten of the sixteen companies were able to negotiate a de minimis settlement with the EPA since together they were responsible for only 3.1 percent of the total wastes at the site. They agreed to pay the federal government $2,586,228 and New Jersey $287,359 for their response costs at the site. The parties also agreed to pay $161,220 to the state for natural resources damage.

The settlement agreement, however, stated that either the state or federal government may seek additional funds from the ten parties if future information shows that they contributed additional wastes, or if the total remediation costs of the site exceed $94 million. The EPA estimated future costs to be $26 million onsite and $20 million offsite. As of this writing, the Justice Department and the EPA were pursuing the other six non-de minimis parties for the remainder of the response costs and all future costs.

Maxey Flats Nuclear Disposal Site

A third case concerned the Maxey Flats nuclear disposal site in Morehead, Kentucky, where over 400 of the 500 named PRPs were listed as having contributed one-tenth of 1 percent of the wastes or less. (Ruhl 1988: 36) The EPA rejected a settlement offer by over seventy SVCs. The EPA's rationale was that the offer was premature, since a site remedy had not been selected, final waste contribution figures had not been established, and the criteria for de minimis standing had not yet been developed.

CONCLUSION

The clean-up liability faced by smaller generators of hazardous wastes is virtually inescapable and potentially significant in cost. Liability is strict, joint, and several, meaning that even the most conscientious smaller generator that has not violated any laws and used only permitted treatment, storage, or disposal facilities (TSDFs) may be held responsible for clean-up costs. Very small quantity generators that are conditionally exempt from the federal regulations that apply to SQGs are not shielded from potential site clean-up liability.

While the new de minimis policy can be a tremendous benefit to smaller generators that are able to negotiate a settlement limiting their liability exposure, it is not a panacea for several reasons. Settlement negotiations will most likely remain lengthy, tedious, and costly. Second, in order to convince the government to agree to a settlement, de minimis waste contributors will most likely have to "cash out" at an amount significantly higher than would be commensurate with the volume of waste disposed. Reopener provisions may negate the advantages of a potential settlement. Should the government refuse to provide smaller generators with a broad release from future liability, the smaller generators might find negotiating an absolute settlement with major waste contributors to their advantage.

In addition, potential conflict between de minimis parties and major waste contributors will remain a reality, and the EPA's decision to enter or not enter into a settlement agreement is not judicially reviewable, which leaves potential settlements with smaller generators at the whim of the EPA. The agency is also free to take action at variance with the newly developed policy. Finally, the determination of who is a de minimis contributor is made on a case-by-case basis, giving smaller generators no hard and fast rule upon which they can depend.

Despite these negatives, there are steps that can be taken by SQGs to minimize their liability over and above being prepared to argue for de minimis status should a lawsuit be filed against them. First, such generators should use permitted TSDFs to reduce the likelihood of future remedial action being required. Smaller generators may want to follow the lead of larger generators and instigate waste reduction processes. In this way the volume of hazardous wastes produced in the first place can be reduced. Finally, smaller generators may want to consider using TSDFs that are frequented by larger generators. Thus, if remediation is required, the likelihood of the smaller generator qualifying as a de minimis contributor may be increased. In addition, larger generators often perform their own inspections of commercial TSDFs to verify compliance by the operators and to assure the generator that liability risks are being minimized (Deyle 1985: 22).

NOTES

1. Pursuant to RCRA regulations promulgated in November 1986, the disposal of perchloroethylene on or into land is now banned.

2. 42 U.S.C.A. 9607. See *United States v. NEPACCO*, 579 F. Supp. 823 (W.D. Mo. 1984); *United States v. Ward*, 618 F. Supp. 884 (D.C. N.C. 1985); *United States v. Wade*, 577 F. Supp. 1326 (E.D. Pa. 1983); *United States v. SCRDI*, 21 Env't Rep. Cas. at 1756 (D. S.C. 1984); *Conservation Chemical Co.*, 619 F. Supp. 162 (W.D. Mo. 1985).

3. 42 U.S.C.A. 9601. See *United States v. Argent Corp.* 21 Env't Rep. Cas. 1354 (D. N.M. 1984); *United States v. Cauffman*, 21 Env't Rep. Cas. 2167 (C.D. Cal. 1984); *New York v. Shore Realty Corp.*, 759 F.2d 1032 (2d Cir. 1985); *Conservation Chemical Co.*, 619 F. Supp. 162 (W.D. Mo. 1985); *Levin Metals Corp. v. Parr-Richmond Terminal Co.*, 25 Env't Rep. Cas. 2113 (9th Cir. 1987); *United States v. SCRDI*, 21 Env't Rep. Cas. at 1581 (D. S.C. 1984); *Maryland Bank and Trust Co.*, 632 F. Supp. 573 (D. Md. 1986); *United States v. Mirabile*, 23 Env't. Rep. Cas. 1511 (E.D. Pa. 1985); *United States v. Carolawn*, 21 Env't Rep. Cas. at 2131 (D. S.C. 1984); *United States v. Cauffman*, 21 Env't Rep. Cas. 2167 (C.D. Cal. 1984); *In Re: T.P. Long Chemical, Inc.*, 45 B.R. 278 (Bkrtcy. Ohio 1985); *Artesian Water Company v. New Castle*, 605 F. Supp. 1348 (D. Del. 1987); *United States v. NEPACCO*, 579 F. Supp. at 848 n.29 (W.D. Mo. 1984).

4. 42 U.S.C.A. 9607. See: *United States v. Ward*, 618 F. Supp. at 894 (D.C. N.C. 1985); *United States v. A&F Materials, Inc.*, 582 F. Supp. 842 (S.D. Ill. 1984); *New York v. General Electric*, 592 F. Supp. at 297 (N.D. N.Y. 1984); *United States v. Conservation Chemical Co.*, 619 F. Supp. 162 (W.D. Mo. 1985); *United States v. Wade*, 577 F. Supp. at 1332 (E.D. Pa. 1983); *United States v. SCRDI*, 21 Env't. Rep. Cas. at 1756 (D. S.C. 1984); *Ottati & Goss*, 23 Env't. Rep. Cas. at 1739 (D. N.H. 1984); *Missouri v. Independent Petrochemical Corp.*, 610 F. Supp. 4 (E.D. Mo. 1985); *Violet v. Picillo*, 25 Env't. Rep. Cas. 1319 (D. R.I. 1986). But see: *Ohio v. Georgeoff*, 562 F. Supp. 1300 (N.D. Ohio 1983).

5. See *United States v. Conservation Chemical Co.*, 619 F. Supp. 162 (W.D. Mo. 1985); *Ottati & Goss*, 23 Env't Rep. Cas. at 1733 (D. N.H. 1984); *United States v. Reilly Tar*, 546 F. Supp. at 1109 (D. Minn. 1982); *United States v. NEPACCO*, 579 F. Supp. at 846 n. 28 (W.D. Mo. 1984); *United States v. Waste Ind.*, 734 F. 2d 159 (4th Cir. 1984). *United States v. Seymour Recycling Corp.*, 618 F. Supp. 1 (S.D. Ind. 1984); *United States v. Vertac Chemical Corp.*, 489 F. Supp. 870 (E.D. Ark. 1980); *United States v. Hardage*, 18 Env't. Rep. Cas. 1685 (W.D. Okla. 1982). But see: *Outmarine Marine Corp. v. Thomas*, 773 F.2d 883 (7th Cir. 1985).

6. 42 U.S.C.A. 9601 (32). See *United States v. M/V Big Sam*, 681 F.2d 432 (5th Cir. 1982); *United States v. Lebeouf Bros. Towing Co.*, 621 F.2d 787 (5th Cir. 1980), cert. denied, 452 U.S. 906 (1981); *Steuart Transportation Co. v. Allied Towing Corp.*, 596 F.2d 906 (4th Cir. 1979); *Burgess v. M/V Tamano*, 564 F.2d 964 (1st Cir. 1977), cert. denied. 435 U.S. 941 (1978); *United States v. Bear Marine Services*, 509 F. Supp. 710 (E.D. La. 1980), reversed on other grounds, 696 F.2d 1117 (5th Cir. 1983); *United States v. Tex Tow*, 598 F.2d 1310 (7th Cir. 1978); *United States v. Ward*, 618 F. Supp. 884 (D.C. N.C. 1985); *United States v. Mirabile*, slip op. at 4 (E.D. Pa. Sept. 4, 1985); *New York v. Shore Realty*, 759 F.2d 1032 (2d Cir. 1985); *United States v. Conservation Chemical Co.*, 619 F. Supp. 162 (W.D. Mo. 1985); *United States v. SCRDI*, 21 Env't. Rep. Cas. at 1756 n.2 (D. S.C. 1984); *United States v. Price*, 577 F. Supp. 1103 (D. IN.J. 1983); *United States v. NEPACCO*, 579 F. Supp. at 843 (W.D. Mo. 1984); *United States*

v. Chem-Dyne Corp., 572 F. Supp. 802 (S.D. Ohio 1983); *City of Philadelphia v. Stephan Chemical Co.*, 544 F. Supp. 1135 (E.D. Pa. 1982); *United States v. Argent Corp.*, 21 Env't. Rep. Cas. 1354 (D. N.M. 1984); *United States v. Cauffman*, 21 Env't. Rep. Cas. 2167 (C.D. Cal. 1984); *United States v. Dickerson et al.*, 640 F. Supp. 448 (D. Md. 1986); *In Re: T.P. Long Chemical, Inc.*, 45 B.R. 278 (Bkrtcy. Ohio 1985); *United States v. Ottati & Goss*, 23 Env't. Rep. Cas. 1705 (D. N.H. 1985); *United States v. Miami Drum Services, Inc.*, 25 Env't. Rep. Cas. 1469 (S.D. Fla. 1986); *Violet v. Picillo*, 25 Env't. Rep. Cas. 1319 (D. R.I. 1986); *United States v. Tyson*, 25 Env't. Rep. Cas. 1899 (E.D. Pa. 1986). But see: *United States v. Wade*, 546 F. Supp. at 792–94.

7. See *United States v. SCRDI*, 21 Env't. Rep. Cas. at 1759 (D. S.C. 1984); *Ottati & Goss*, 23 Env't. Rep. Cas. 1705 (D. N.H. 1985); *United States v. A&F Materials, Inc.*, 578 F. Supp. at 1249 (S.D. Ill. 1984); *United States v. NEPACCO*, 579 F. Supp. at 845 (W.D. Mo. 1984); *United States v. Dickerson*, 640 F. Supp. 448 (D. Md. 1986); *United States v. Northernaire Plating Co.*, No. G84–1113CA7 (W.D. Mich. May 5, 1987).

8. See *United States v. Mirable*, slip op. at 4, 14 ELR 20992 (E.D. Pa. Sept. 4, 1985); *United States v. SCRDI*, 21 Env't. Rep. Cas. at 1759 (D. S.C. 1984); *United States v. Chem-Dyne*, 572 F. Supp. at 811 (S.D. Ohio 1983); *United States v. Conservation Chemical Co.*, 619 F. Supp. 162 (W.D. Mo. 1985); 589 F. Supp. at 63 (W.D. Mo. 1984); *United States v. A&F Materials, Inc.*, 578 F. Supp. at 1249 (S.D. Ill. 1984); *United States v. NEPACCO*, 579 F. Supp. at 845 (W.D. Mo. 1984); *United States v. Ottati & Goss*, 23 Env't. Rep. Cas. at 1733 (D. N.H. 1985); *New York v. Shore Realty* 759 F.2d 1032 (2d Cir. 1985); *United States v. Ward*, 618 F. Supp. 884 (E.D. N.C. 1985); *United States v. Shell Oil Company*, 605 F. Supp. 1064 at 1083–84 n. 9 (D. Colo. 1985); *United States v. Miami Drum Services, Inc.*, 25 Env't. Rep. Cas. at 1474 (S.D. Fla. 1985). But see: *United States v. Stringfellow*, 20 Env't. Rep. Cas. 1905 (C.D. Cal. 1984).

9. See *United States v. Ottati & Goss*, 23 Env't. Rep. Cas. at 1734 (D. N.H. 1985); *United States v. A&F Materials, Inc.* 578 F. Supp. at 1249 (S.D. Ill. 1984); *United States v. South Carolina Recycling and Disposal, Inc.*, 20 Env't. Rep. Cas. at 1759 (D. S.C. 1984); *United States v. Wade*, 546 F. Supp. at 792 (E.D. Pa. 1983); *United States v. NEPACCO*, 579 F. Supp. at 845 (W.D. Mo. 1984); *United States v. Dickerson*, 640 F. Supp. 448 (D. Md. 1986); *United States v. Northernaire Plating Co.*, No. G84–1113CA7 (W.D. Mich. 1987).

10. In 1980, when the EPA first promulgated regulations pursuant to RCRA, small quantity generators, then defined as those businesses producing less than 1,000 kilograms (2,200 pounds) of hazardous waste in a calendar month, were exempted from most regulations. In November 1984, however, the Hazardous and Solid Waste Amendments to RCRA were signed into law. Under the new law, Congress ordered the EPA to regulate smaller generators that produce between 100 and 1,000 kilograms of hazardous waste in a calendar month. Most of the smaller generator regulations promulgated by the EPA pursuant to the 1984 amendments became effective on September 22, 1986.

11. 42 U.S.C.A. 9607 (b) sets forth the following defenses: an act of God; an act of war; an act or omission of a third party other than an employee or agent of the defendant, or than one whose act or omission occurs in connection with a contractual relationship (with exceptions); or any combination of the above. See:

United States v. Ward, 618 F. Supp. 884 (E.D. N.C. 1985); *New York v. Shore Realty*, 759 F.2d at 1044 (2d Cir. 1985); *United States v. Cauffman*, 21 Env't. Rep. Cas. 2167 (C.D. Cal. 1984); *United States v. Milliken*, slip op. at 4 (D. S.C. 1986); *United States v. SCRDI*, 20 Env't. Rep. Cas. at 1756 (D. S.C. 1984); *United States v. Reilly Tar & Chemical Co.*, 546 F. Supp. 1100, 1118 (D. Minn. 1982); *Pinole Point Properties v. Bethlehem Steel Corp.*, 596 F. Supp. 283 (N.D. Cal. 1984); *United States v. Argent Corp.*, 21 Env't. Rep. Cas. 1356 (D. N.M. 1984); *United States v. Price*, 577 F. Supp. 1103 (D. N.J. 1983); *United States v. Cramblit*, slip op. at 3 (E.D. Cal. 1984); *Mola Development Corp. v. United States*, 22 Env't. Rep. Cas. 1443 (C.D. Cal. 1985). But see: *Mardan Corp. v. C.G.C. Music, Ltd.*, 804 F.2d 1454 (9th Cir. 1986); *United States v. Conservation Chemical Co.*, 619 F. Supp. 162 (W.D. Mo. 1985); *Violet v. Picillo*, 648 F. Supp. 1283 (D. R.I. 1986); *United States v. Hardage*, 26 Env't. Rep. Cas. 1049 (W.D. Okla. 1987).

12. See EPA Interim Guidance, 52 *Federal Register* 24333, June 30, 1987. See also 52 *Federal Register* 43393, November 12, 1987.

13. Id.

14. Id.

15. The "value of a present sum certain" is defined as how much a payment by a party is worth now, compared to its probable worth in the future. Factors such as inflation, risks, and time are often considered in calculating the value of a present sum certain.

16. See note 12, supra.

5

Adherence to Small Quantity Generator Regulations

The preceding chapters provide a basis for anticipating what factors will likely influence decisions made by smaller generators in response to federal and state regulations governing hazardous waste management. This chapter presents the results of the author's analysis of factors associated with compliance behavior by smaller generators in New Jersey. The analysis focuses on both the calculative costs and benefits of compliance decisions and some of the organizational factors that may mitigate how decision makers behave. I also examine the role of hazardous waste liability in decisions to adhere to state and federal hazardous waste regulations. Since the hazardous wastes produced by conditionally exempt VSQGs may also pose a threat to human health and the environment, their behavior is examined as well as that of the regulated SQGs.

The chapter begins with an overview of what has been deduced about constraints on SQG compliance from casual observation, anecdotal evidence, and descriptive studies of smaller generator waste management. The majority of the chapter is devoted to discussing the results and implications of the New Jersey study, which was based on a survey of smaller generators.

APPARENT CONSTRAINTS ON SQG COMPLIANCE

There is virtually universal agreement that the major constraint on hazardous waste regulatory compliance by SQGs is lack of knowledge of the applicable regulations and of how to comply with them. These constraints are attributed to limited expertise and staff and a reluctance to hire specialized legal or technical advisors (Jones 1984: 8; Josephson 1984: 156A; Schwartz et al. 1987: 19).

The author conducted a small survey in April 1984 to generate preliminary hypotheses about the determinants of regulatory compliance behavior by hazardous waste generators (Deyle 1985). Interviews were conducted with fourteen hazardous waste generators and six waste management consultants in central New York State. The surveyed firms represented a broad cross-section of generators based on firm size, industry and waste types, waste volumes, corporate structure, and location (rural, suburban, and urban).

Most waste managers interviewed claimed to be familiar with the hazardous waste regulations. Out of twelve waste managers who responded, ten indicated that they were very familiar or generally familiar with sanctions for noncompliance, and two said that they were not very familiar. Those who claimed to be very or generally familiar cited both financial and criminal penalties, and many suggested that they would be held personally responsible, either for criminal penalties or by their employers if financial penalties were levied against their firms. There was no apparent relationship between firm or respondent characteristics and the reported degree of familiarity with sanctions for noncompliance.

One of the waste management consultants surveyed in the central New York study maintained that many firms are not fully aware of the regulatory requirements for proper waste identification, container labeling, and manifesting. Another estimated that only 25 percent of the firms in New York State were in full compliance at that time with standards for onsite hazardous waste storage and contingency plans. On the other hand, this respondent also suggested that very few firms were operating entirely outside of state and federal regulation.

Abt Associates, in a qualitative study of SQGs in New York State performed under subcontract with Environmental Resources Management, Inc., found that many SQGs are unfamiliar with what wastes are regulated as hazardous (ERM 1985: 31). Wu et al. (1984) reported similar results from a survey of 100 SQGs in Mecklenburg and Gaston counties, North Carolina. Fifteen percent of the firms surveyed indicated that they did not know which federal or state hazardous waste regulations pertained to their operations.

CONSAD Research Corporation, in a survey of small businesses subject to federal environmental regulations, found that almost all firms with more than fifty employees considered themselves to be "very well informed" or "somewhat well informed" about applicable environmental regulations. Among businesses with twenty to forty-nine employees, 67 percent claimed to be informed, while only 50 percent of businesses with fewer than twenty employees made such a claim (Steger et al. 1983: 2.59, 2.44). Respondents who indicated that they were "somewhat well informed" claimed only to be familiar with the regulatory programs rather than being knowledgeable about actual requirements and compliance procedures.

A 1985 survey of VSQGs by the Association of Bay Area Governments in California found that 51 percent of the firms interviewed were not familiar with state or federal hazardous waste regulations and only 22 percent indicated that they were somewhat familiar (Russell and Meiorin 1985). A 1983 hazardous waste management survey by the Smaller Business Association of New England (SBANE) gathered information from 161 small manufacturing firms of which 81 generated hazardous wastes. While 38 percent of the respondents who were waste generators claimed that they were somewhat familiar with federal and state hazardous waste regulations, and 54 percent said that they were familiar, 89 percent indicated that they would like more information about how the regulations apply to their own operations (SBANE 1983: 2–3).

Sanction severity was almost universally perceived as high by the central New York waste managers (Deyle 1985), yet most of them ranked the level of enforcement as low (nine of twelve respondents). Those firms that had been inspected by the EPA or the State Department of Environmental Conservation tended to rank the enforcement level as "high," although two waste managers for larger firms (1,200 to 1,400 employees) ranked enforcement as low despite having been inspected. There may be a relationship between firm size and perception of enforcement levels. Smaller firms are less likely to be subject to regular compliance inspections for other regulatory programs and may, therefore, be more likely to rank the enforcement level as high after being inspected once or twice in the course of a year.

Some of the smaller firms contacted in the central New York survey expressed uncertainty as to their complete compliance with the regulations and indicated that they had inadequate time and expertise to comprehend and stay abreast of changes in the regulations. Several firms, including larger ones, indicated that they had had difficulty complying with requirements for training of waste handling personnel and development of proper accident contingency plans.

Several of the waste management consultants interviewed suggested that firms with limited environmental expertise resources are more likely to have difficulty coping with the complexity of federal and state hazardous waste regulations and attaining full compliance. Several of the consultants also suggested that smaller firms with limited financial resources are less likely to make capital investments to achieve regulatory compliance unless they perceive a strong likelihood of enforcement.

Wu et al. (1984) found that most firms did not have the technical staff needed to monitor pertinent regulations and assess regulatory obligations and management options. In 1985, the Rockefeller Institute of Government conducted a survey of New York State hazardous waste generators and trade associations. One trade association representative interviewed by the institute said that most small-business owners and operators do not even attempt to read the full text of hazardous waste laws or regulations because of their complexity (Palmer et al. 1986: 88). Nemeth and Kamperman (1985: 23) report that many of the information calls responded to through the Georgia Tech technical assistance program for SQGs concerned interpretations of the regulations. The staff of the New Jersey Department of Environmental Protection Hazardous Waste Advisement Program also reports a preponderance of technical assistance questions concerning specific regulations (Gashlin 1986).

Many SQGs that ship their wastes offsite for disposal are unaware of how the hazardous wastes are actually managed. In the SBANE survey, 25 percent of respondents who were generators indicated that they did not know where their hazardous wastes were disposed (SBANE 1983: 3). In the 1985 national survey of smaller generators, 13 percent of the generators contacted did not know how their wastes were ultimately disposed after being shipped offsite (Ruder et al. 1985: 39). In the 1984 survey conducted by Wu et al. in North Carolina, 54 percent of the SQGs interviewed did not know where the hazardous wastes were ultimately disposed.

Nemeth and Kamperman (1985: 10) indicate that most firms they assisted through the Georgia Tech technical assistance program "had no real concept of waste management, let alone details of their waste streams." The CONSAD study reports that even when small-business operators are aware of educational and technical assistance services available from the federal EPA, they frequently do not have the resources to make use of them (Steger et al. 1983: 2.7).

Schwartz et al. (1987) suggest that small-business management decisions are based primarily on short-term economic factors; therefore, most SQGs are unlikely to be responsive to regulatory sanctions. The small-business decisionmaking studies reviewed in Chapter 2 support the assumption of limited long-term planning and strategic planning by small businesses. There is no evidence, however, to support or refute the contention that regulatory sanctions are viewed as long-term rather than short-term costs. A short-range planning horizon is likely, however, to minimize the level of concern SQGs would have with the long-term liability associated with hazardous waste generation and management.

Several authors have suggested that high compliance costs are a significant disincentive to compliance by SQGs. Josephson (1984) notes that transportation costs can be prohibitively high for smaller generators. Because transporters charge a considerable fee for waste pickup regardless of the volume collected, the cost per ton is very high when the generator produces only a few 55-gallon drums per month. For example, the total cost for transport and disposal for a single drum can be as high as $600, while the price per drum for ten drums of the same waste would be in the range of $60 to $181 and for forty drums could be as low as $31 to $166 per drum (Schwartz et al. 1987: 18). Compliance costs may also constitute a more significant drain on capital for small businesses that are only marginally profitable and operating in highly competitive markets (Josephson 1984: 156A).

Many of the VSQGs that have obtained EPA identification numbers and are using the manifest system are doing so because transporters or sanitary landfills have refused to take the wastes, despite their conditionally exempt regulatory status (Deyle 1985; Katz 1988: 68). It has also been suggested that some VSQGs have been motivated to use the manifest system and permitted hazardous waste disposal facilities because of concern with potential clean-up liability (Katz 1988: 68).

These studies lend support to the conclusions drawn at the end of Chapter 3. Compliance by smaller generators appears to be constrained by limited knowledge of the regulations, limited time on the part of small-business decision makers, and limited access to technical and legal expertise. The cost of compliance may also be a deterrent to some smaller generators, while the short-term planning horizon of many small businesses may preclude serious consideration of long-term liability costs. In the study of New Jersey smaller generators conducted by the author, waste managers were asked to rank a list of possible constraints on compliance with hazardous waste regulations. Their responses are presented in a subsequent section following a description of the survey study and characterization of the respondents.

THE NEW JERSEY SMALLER GENERATOR SURVEY

The New Jersey study was conducted in 1985 by the Technology and Information Policy Program (TIPP) at Syracuse University for the New Jersey Hazardous Waste Facilities Siting Commission. It consisted of a cross-sectional mailed survey of 1,000 businesses in the major smaller generator industries. One of the principal objectives of the survey was to determine what factors contribute to regulatory compliance by SQGs and to voluntary adherence to hazardous waste regulations by VSQGs.

The Survey Sample

The survey sample was stratified to include 300 firms in the state hazardous waste regulatory program and 700 firms outside the program.

Firms in the regulatory program were selected from the state's data base of establishments that had manifested shipments of hazardous wastes to treatment or disposal facilities during the period 1983 through 1985. The sample was stratified to include 150 VSQGs and 150 SQGs from among approximately 1,450 smaller generators in the manifest system. The non-manifest subsample of 700 firms was drawn at random from approximately 41,000 firms in the smaller generator SIC codes in the state. New Jersey Department of Labor unemployment insurance name and address files for the first quarter of 1985 were used to identify these firms.

The fraction of establishments actually qualifying as VSQGs or SQGs within these SIC codes was anticipated to be between 19 and 32 percent (Bozeman et al. 1986b). Usable questionnaires were received from a total of 414 respondents. Seventy of the respondents qualified as VSQGs while 106 were SQGs. The remaining respondents did not generate hazardous wastes. The proportion of VSQGs and SQGs from the nonmanifest sample was 22 percent, which falls within the expected range. Details concerning survey administration, the pretest, and response bias analyses are included in Appendix A.

Smaller Generator Characteristics

The average respondent from the total sample of firms that generated hazardous wastes was the owner, president, or other upper-level manager of a private-sector, relatively small firm of about sixty employees. The typical respondent firm earned modest profits in 1985 and was in the vehicle maintenance or metal manufacturing industrial sector. The median firm size was eighteen employees for the pooled sample of respondents from the manifest and nonmanifest samples. The significant difference between mean and median firm size is attributable to the presence in the sample of several relatively large firms with between 400 and 2,000 employees despite qualifying as SQGs or VSQGs.

The typical respondent was similar for the SQGs and VSQGs on all dimensions except firm size and industry type. The ranges of variation within the full sample and for the SQGs and VSQGs in the sample for the different respondent characteristics are presented in Tables 5.1 through 5.4. As shown in Table 5.1, SQGs are typically larger than VSQGs with median sizes of 25 and 10.5 employees respectively. A t-test of medians confirms the significance of this apparent difference ($t = 3.2662$, $df = 166$, $p = 0.00$).[1]

More of the respondents from VSQGs were owners or other chief executive officers than were those from SQGs, but the difference is not statistically significant ($X^2 = 1.658$, $df = 1$, $p = 0.20$).[2] A larger proportion of VSQG firms had sustained a loss during the preceding year

Table 5.1
Number of Employees of Respondent Organization

Employment Measure	VSQG	SQG	Pooled
Mean	70	49	58
Median	10.5	25	18
Minimum	1	2	1
Maximum	2000	400	2000

Table 5.2
Job Category of Respondent

Job Category	VSQG	SQG	Pooled
Owner	40%	30%	34%
President or other upper-level management	22%	23%	22%
Operating manager or engineer	30%	35%	33%
Parent firm manager or engineer	3%	2%	2%
Secretary or office manager	4%	5%	5%
Other	1%	5%	4%

than SQG firms, but again the difference is not significant ($X^2 = 1.730$, df $= 2$, p $= 0.42$).

There are some noteworthy differences in industry group between the SQGs and VSQGs as shown in Table 5.4, particularly for the following groups: laundries, metal manufacturing, printing and ceramics, analytic and clinical labs, and secondary SIC codes. Chi-square analysis of an aggregated categorization of industry groups indicates that these differences are significant ($X^2 = 19.587$, df $= 5$, p $= 0.00$).

These comparisons suggest that the VSQG and SQG populations are considerably different on at least two levels and may, therefore, be ex-

Table 5.3
Profitability of Respondent Organization

Profitability	VSQG	SQG	Pooled
Severe to Modest Losses	24%	16%	19%
Modest Profits	57%	66%	62%
Good to Excellent Profits	19%	18%	19%

pected to behave somewhat differently in terms of their waste management practices. Any comparisons of the voluntary adherence behavior of VSQGs with the compliance behavior of SQGs should take these differences into account.

REPORTED COMPLIANCE CONSTRAINTS

In the New Jersey survey, smaller generators were asked to rank the importance of a list of factors as constraints on compliance with state and federal laws and regulations governing waste management. The constraint rankings included the following: very important constraint, somewhat important constraint, a constraint but not important, and not a constraint. A frequency distribution for the responses is presented in Table 5.5, in which the last two constraint categories are combined.

The constraints most frequently ranked as very important include regulatory complexity or inflexibility, technical difficulty of determining if wastes qualify as hazardous, the cost of transportation and treatment or disposal at permitted facilities, and the cost of waste management consultants. These are followed by lack of time to stay informed of applicable regulations and unavailability of hazardous waste management technical expertise within the respondent's organization. There is a significant split, however, in rankings of expertise factors. Forty-nine percent of the respondents ranked the high cost of consultants as not important or not a constraint, and 55 percent similarly ranked lack of in-house expertise.

Lack of time was the most prevalent factor ranked as a somewhat important constraint followed by access to hazardous waste management technology information, regulatory complexity and inflexibility, and the cost of transportation and treatment or disposal at permitted facilities.

Table 5.4
Industry Group of Respondent Organization

Industry Group	VSQG	SQG	Pooled
Pesticide Application Services	1%	0%	1%
Chemical Manufacturing	0%	2%	1%
Formulators	0%	0%	0%
Laundries	0%	12%	7%
Other Services	1%	0%	1%
Photography	0%	0%	0%
Vehicle Maintenance	49%	53%	51%
Equipment Repair	0%	0%	0%
Metal Manufacturing	12%	20%	19%
Construction	1%	1%	1%
Furniture/Wood Manufacture & Refinishing	1%	1%	1%
Printing/Ceramics	7%	4%	5%
Cleaning Agents & Cosmetics Manufacturers	0%	0%	0%
Other Manufacturng	1%	3%	2%
Paper Industry	0%	1%	1%
Analytic & Clinical Laboratories	6%	2%	4%
Educational & Vocational Shops	1%	0%	1%
Wholesale & Retail Trades	0%	0%	0%
Secondary SIC Codes	14%	0%	6%

Table 5.5
Respondent Ranking of Compliance Constraints

Importance Rank Frequencies

Compliance Constraint	Very Important	Somewhat Important	Not a Constraint or Not Important
High cost of consultants	28%	23%	49%
Lack of in-house expertise	25%	20%	55%
Cost of waste determinations	22%	26%	53%
Difficulty of waste determinations	41%	30%	29%
Identifying treatment and disposal facilities	21%	24%	55%
Identifying transporters	20%	25%	56%
Access to information	18%	35%	47%
Regulatory complexity & inflexibility	43%	34%	23%
High cost of transportation, and treatment and disposal	34%	32%	34%
Lack of time	25%	50%	24%

FACTORS RELATED TO COMPLIANCE BEHAVIOR

The respondents' rankings of compliance constraints are consistent with the conclusions drawn from the qualitative studies discussed previously. One of the major objectives of the New Jersey survey was to go beyond a subjective assessment of compliance constraints to assess the relation-

Table 5.6
Measures of Adherence to New Jersey Hazardous Waste Regulations

Measure	Description
Manifest Use	Use of the state manifest system to record shipments of hazardous waste from the point of generation to offsite facilities for treatment or disposal
Contingency Plan Maintenance	Preparation and maintenance of a written hazardous waste accident contigency plan
Employee Training Program	Training of employees who handle hazardous wastes

ship between actual behavior and variables that could be altered by public policies and programs. The intent was to assess the extent to which compliance behavior can be explained by rational compliance variables, such as sanction severity and certainty as well as such organizational variables as knowledge and expertise constraints and firm financial condition. The analysis was concerned with both regulatory compliance by SQGs and with voluntary adherence to hazardous waste regulations by VSQGs.

The following sections describe the survey variables that were used in the analysis, the analyses that were performed, and the findings.

Survey Measures

Three questions were asked to measure voluntary adherence to and compliance with requirements of the New Jersey hazardous waste regulations. The three dependent measures are listed in Table 5.6. The individual questions are reproduced in Appendixes B and C. All three measures were assessed with yes or no questions.

New Jersey regulations require that all generators of 100 kilograms or more of hazardous waste per month use an official state manifest form when shipping hazardous wastes offsite to other facilities for storage, treatment, recycling, or disposal (New Jersey Administrative Code 7:26–7.3, 7.4). Adherence to the manifest requirements can be unambiguously defined: a generator either uses the manifest system or does not. While one might differentiate levels of compliance with the manifest system based on correct filing of manifests and recordkeeping, such violations are regarded as minor by the enforcement agencies. Therefore, the fact that a SQG firm was in the state manifest system was used as the measure of compliance with the manifest regulatory requirement. Any VSQG in the system was classified as voluntarily adhering to the regulations.

Generators of 100 or more kilograms per month are also required to prepare and maintain written hazardous waste accident contingency plans that describe the actions to be taken by personnel in the event of a fire, explosion, or other unplanned release of hazardous waste into the environment (New Jersey Administrative Code 7: 26–9.7). These generators, which include SQGs and large quantity generators, are also required to provide on-the-job or classroom training to employees who handle hazardous wastes (New Jersey Administrative Code 7: 26–9.4(g)).

Adherence to contingency plan requirements and to employee training requirements was measured in the survey through self-report questions. Reliance on self-report data for these two dependent variables raises some validity concerns. Analyses of the validity of self-report data for individual criminal behavior indicate, however, that survey responses can be 80 to 90 percent accurate (Tittle 1980: 29–30).

Table 5.7 presents the variables included in the analysis that were anticipated to be related to compliance and voluntary regulatory adherence behavior. The survey included three measures of the calculative cost of noncompliance: perceived maximum fine, estimated legal fees, and liability concern. Liability concern served as a proxy for the perceived magnitude of a firm's liability exposure from failure to manage its hazardous wastes in accordance with state and federal regulations. Rosemary O'Leary described the actual liability of smaller generators in the preceding chapter.

The calculative cost of compliance with (or voluntary adherence to) the regulations was measured as the respondent's perception of the administrative cost of adhering to the regulations. An open-ended question asked respondents to estimate the probability of apprehension. The cost of subsequent compliance was derived from an open-ended measure of enforcement delay that was multiplied by the apprehension probability value and the administrative cost estimate to produce a discounted cost of compliance following an enforcement action.

A series of true-false questions measured respondents' knowledge of applicable state hazardous waste regulations and legal liability. Three liability knowledge questions concerned the application of strict liability derived from case law under the federal Superfund law, to hazardous waste generation and management practices. A composite measure of liability knowledge was developed with a Guttman scale.

Access to and use of legal and environmental management expertise in hazardous waste management decisionmaking were measured with a question that asked respondents to rank their use of several information sources: in-house legal experts, environmental consultants, and in-house environmental experts. The ranking scale was as follows: never/not avail-

Table 5.7
Anticipated Determinants of Smaller Generator Adherence to Hazardous Waste Regulations

Measure	Description
Fine	Perceived maximum civil fine a generator would be subject to for failure to use the state manifest system
Legal Fees	Estimated legal fees and other costs to defend an organization in an enforcement action brought by the state for allegedly failing to use the state manifest system
Liability Concern	Extent of the respondent organization's concern with the legal liability attending hazardous waste generation and management
Administrative Cost	Perceived annual cost of completing the necessary paper work and other administrative tasks involved in using the state manifest system
Apprehension Probability	Estimation of the percentage of organizations not complying with state hazardous waste regulations that were detected and prosecuted during the previous year
Enforcement Delay	Perceived delay between detection of a violation of the state's hazardous waste regulations and initiation of an enforcement action
Knowledge of Liability for Transporter Actions	Knowledge that under strict liability a generator can be held liable for damages resulting from actions of a second party waste transporter
Knowledge of Liability for Facility Actions	Knowledge that under strict liability a generator can be held liable for damages resulting from actions of a second party waste treatment or disposal facility
Knowledge of Strict Liability	Knowledge that under strict liability a generator can be held indefinitely liable for damages regardless of how wastes are managed
Composite Liability Knowledge	Guttman-scaled composite of knowledge of liability for transporter actions, facility actions, and strict liability
Regulatory Knowledge	Knowledge of the 100 kg/mo regulatory exemption threshold for VSQGs
In-House Legal Experts	Access to or use of in-house or parent company lawyers in waste management decisionmaking
In-House Environmental Experts	Access to or use of in-house or parent company environmental managers or engineers in waste management decisionmaking
Environmental Consultants	Access to or use of environmental management or engineering consultants in waste management decisionmaking

Table 5.7 (continued)
Anticipated Determinants of Smaller Generator Adherence to Hazardous Waste Regulations

Measure	Description
Firm Profitability	Self-reports of firm profitability in 1985 based on an ordinal scale: (1) severe to moderate losses, (2) modest profits, or (3) good to excellent profits
Firm Size	Number of employees
Owner or Other Executive Officer	Indicator variable based on job title

able, sometimes, and often. Use of these sources of expertise was measured with this three-level ordinal scale. The last two categories (sometimes and often) were aggregated to yield an indicator variable that measured access to expertise.

Analysis of the Survey Data

Analysis of the survey responses included bivariate correlation analysis, using Kendall's tau-b rank order correlation measure, and logit multivariate regression analysis. Nonresponses and "don't know" responses to individual questions reduced the VSQG sample to less than thirty for multivariate analysis. Therefore, the voluntary adherence analysis was limited to bivariate correlations between hypothesized independent variables and the three dependent variables. Two multivariate models developed through an exploratory analytic process were tested in a logit analysis of compliance by SQGs. Kendall's tau-b correlations were also calculated for the SQG compliance measures and the hypothesized determinants of compliance. In addition, correlations were analyzed between the respondents' rankings of possible compliance constraints and their actual compliance behavior. A detailed discussion of the analytic methods is presented in Appendix A.

Findings from the Survey Analysis

Results of the survey analysis lend support to some of the conclusions from qualitative and descriptive studies of waste management practices by smaller generators. Unfamiliarity with hazardous waste regulations appears to be a significant constraint on compliance by SQGs. Lack of technical expertise and lack of knowledge of the liability associated with hazardous waste generation and management are associated with lower levels of adherence to the regulations by both SQGs and VSQGs. There is also evidence that lack of time, limited access to information, and regulatory complexity are significant constraints on compliance by SQGs. There is no direct evidence that high costs of compliance are significantly associated with lower levels of compliance. It is also apparent that many waste managers in SQG firms do not explicitly consider such factors as sanction severity and certainty or other costs of noncompliance in making decisions about compliance with hazardous waste regulations.

Expertise and Waste Management Decisionmaking

The survey analysis indicates that access to legal and environmental experts and the extent to which they are consulted in hazardous waste management decisionmaking are related to regulatory compliance by SQGs and voluntary adherence to hazardous waste regulations by VSQGs. There are also significant correlations between respondents' rankings of limited in-house expertise as a constraint on compliance and the actual compliance of SQGs with each of the three regulatory requirements as shown in Table 5.8.

The data presented in Table 5.9 indicate that access to and use of in-house legal consultants in hazardous waste management decisionmaking is significantly correlated with voluntary adherence by VSQGs to all three regulatory requirements. Results of the multivariate compliance analyses, which are presented in Table 5.10, indicate that legal expertise is also a significant factor in contingency plan compliance by SQGs. In the case of compliance with manifest requirements, it appears that the use of legal expertise may actually result in less compliance. This finding offers some support for the contention that greater legal expertise may engender recalcitrance rather than compliance.

Access to and use of in-house environmental management experts are positively correlated with voluntary adherence to contingency plan and employee training requirements. The multivariate analyses also indicate a significant, positive relationship between these measures of expertise and compliance with all three regulatory requirements.

Access to or use of environmental consultants is correlated with voluntary adherence by VSQGs to employee training and manifest use requirements, but these variables are not significant in any of the multivariate compliance models. They do, however, exhibit significant bivariate correlations with contingency plan compliance at the 0.05 level of significance (Kendall's tau-b coefficients of 0.24 and 0.25). They are

Table 5.8
Kendall's Tau-b Correlations for Compliance Constraint Rankings and SQG Compliance Behavior

	Compliance Measures		
Compliance Constraint	Contingency Plan	Employee Training	Manifest Use
High Cost of Consultants	-0.06 (0.55)[*]	-0.03 (0.78)	-0.13 (0.25)
Lack of In-House Expertise	-0.27 (0.02)[a]	-0.29 (0.01)[a]	-0.26 (0.03)[a]
Cost of Waste Determinations	-0.09 (0.40)	-0.06 (0.60)	-0.17 (0.15)
Difficulty of Waste Determinations	-0.25 (0.02)[a]	0.00 (0.97)	-0.19 (0.10)
Identifying Treatment and Disposal Facilities	-0.08 (0.44)	-0.04 (0.69)	-0.03 (0.82)
Identifying Transporters	-0.12 (0.28)	-0.02 (0.84)	-0.14 (0.23)
Access to Information	-0.03 (0.77)	0.01 (0.95)	-0.35 (0.00)[a]
Regulatory Complexity & Inflexibility	0.01 (0.91)	0.01 (0.92)	-0.19 (0.10)[b]
High Cost of Transportation, and Treatment and Disposal	0.00 (1.00)	0.04 (0.75)	-0.04 (0.75)
Lack of Time	-0.01 (0.91)	0.05 (0.67)	-0.22 (0.06)[b]

[*]Coefficient probability values are in parentheses.
[a]Significant at 0.05 level.
[b]Significant at 0.10 level.

Table 5.9
Kendall's Tau-b Correlations for Voluntary Regulatory Adherence Variables

	Adherence Measures		
Adherence Determinants	Contingency Plan	Employee Training	Manifest Use
Firm Size	0.15* (0.14)	0.09 (0.39)	0.11 (0.40)
Profitability	0.19 (0.12)	0.22 (0.08)[b]	0.06 (0.67)
Knowledge of Liability for Transporter Actions	0.03 (0.85)	-0.16 (0.24)	0.42 (0.01)[a]
Knowledge of Liability for Facility Actions	0.14 (0.28)	-0.12 (0.37)	0.08 (0.64)
Knowledge of Strict Liability	-0.02 (0.88)	-0.17 (0.29)	0.13 (0.50)
Composite Liability Knowledge	-0.01 (0.96)	-0.09 (0.58)	0.34 (0.07)[b]
Owner or Other Executive Officer	-0.00 (0.97)	-0.21 (0.08)[b]	-0.15 (0.32)
Access to In-House Legal Expertise	0.22 (0.09)[b]	0.27 (0.05)[a]	0.32 (0.05)[a]
Use of In-House Legal Expertise	0.24 (0.07)[b]	0.25 (0.06)[b]	0.32 (0.05)[a]
Access to In-House Environmental Expertise	0.34 (0.01)[a]	0.33 (0.01)[a]	-0.17 (0.29)
Use of In-House Environmental Expertise	0.36 (0.00)[a]	0.32 (0.01)[a]	-0.17 (0.28)
Access to Environmental Consultants	0.18 (0.15)	0.25 (0.05)[a]	0.29 (0.07)[b]
Use of Environmental Consultants	0.17 (0.17)	0.25 (0.05)[a]	0.31 (0.05)[a]
Administrative Cost	0.28 (0.04)[a]	0.50 (0.00)[a]	-0.18 (0.26)
Liability Concern	0.26 (0.02)[a]	0.18 (0.11)	-0.05 (0.73)
Regulatory Knowledge	0.06 (0.76)	0.16 (0.38)	-0.44 (0.05)[a]
Regulatory Familiarity	-0.02 (0.85)	0.00 (0.98)	0.12 (0.42)

*Coefficient probability values are in parentheses.
[a]Significant at 0.05 level.
[b]Significant at 0.10 level.

also correlated at the 0.10 significance level with employee training compliance (Kendall's tau-b coefficients of 0.20 and 0.18). Intercorrelation among the expertise variables may explain the lack of significance of the environmental consultant variables in the multivariate models. Kendall's

Table 5.10
Logit Coefficients for Determinants of Small Quantity Generator Compliance

Compliance Measures

Compliance Determinants	Contingency Plan Model 1	Contingency Plan Model 2*	Employee Training Model 1	Employee Training Model 2*	Manifest Use Model 1	Manifest Use Model 2*
Administrative Cost	1.363[a]	0.967[a]	-0.200	0.082	0.151	0.289
Firm Size	-2.899[a]	-2.074[a]	-0.977[a]	-0.871[a]	1.142	0.864
Profitability	1.607	1.305	1.472[b]	1.053	-4.350[b]	-3.145[a]
Transporter Liability					10.586[b]	7.206[a]
Facility Liability					-5.892	-3.539
Strict Liability	8.112[a]		8.418		-5.129	-5.361[b]
Composite Liability Knowledge	8.595[b]	5.989[a]		1.138[b]		
Owner or Other Executive Officer	7.029[a]	5.898[a]	-1.120	-1.335	-5.861	-5.357[b]
Access to In-House Legal Expertise		5.822[a]	0.006	-0.374		
Use of In-House Legal Expertise					-6.227[a]	-5.311[a]
Access to In-House Environmental Expertise	12.118[a]	8.990[a]	2.047	2.238[b]		
Use of In-House Environmental Expertise					3.148[b]	1.992[b]
Access to Environmental Consultants	2.073		-0.409			
Use of Environmental Consultants					-2.535	
R	0.588	0.586	0.302	0.164	0.320	0.325
Somer's D	0.916	0.889	0.780	0.720	0.884	0.852

[a] significant at 0.05 level.
[b] significant at 0.10 level.
*Model 2 excludes access/use of environmental consultants.

Table 5.11
Kendall's Tau-b Correlations for Expertise Variables

Expertise Determinants	Firm Size	Profit- ability	Owner or Other Executive Officer
Access to In-House Lawyers	0.22* (0.00)[a]	0.12 (0.16)	-0.24 (0.00)[a]
Use of In-House Lawyers	0.21 (0.00)[a]	0.11 (0.18)	-0.23 (0.01)[a]
Access to In-House Environmental Experts	0.15 (0.03)[a]	-0.03 (0.73)	-0.16 (0.06)[b]
Use of In-House Environmental Experts	0.15 (0.03)[a]	-0.02 (0.80)	-0.15 (0.06)[b]
Access to Environmental Management Consultants	0.12 (0.07)[b]	0.08 (0.40)	-0.20 (0.01)[a]
Use of Environmental Management Consultants	0.12 (0.06)[b]	0.06 (0.45)	-0.23 (0.00)[a]

*Coefficient probability values are in parentheses.

[a]Significant at 0.05 level.
[b]Significant at 0.10 level.

tau-b correlations among the expertise variables range from 0.20 to 0.29 with probability values of 0.00 to 0.01.

It is generally assumed that firm expertise in specialized fields is least in the smallest, less financially viable businesses. It is also likely that the use of such experts will be less when management decisionmaking is more centralized. Several of these assumptions are supported by the relationships between expertise and firm size, firm profitability, and the locus of hazardous waste management decisionmaking for both SQGs and VSQGs.

As shown in Table 5.11, larger firms among both SQGs and VSQGs are more likely to have access to or make greater use of in-house and consultant legal and environmental experts. Correlations in Table 5.11 also substantiate the contention that firms with more centralized decisionmaking, at which the owner or other executive officer makes waste management decisions, are less likely to make use of legal or environmental management experts. There is no significant association, however, between firm profitability and access to or use of experts.

Firm and Waste Manager Characteristics

Data in Tables 5.9 and 5.10 indicate that firms are less likely to comply with or voluntarily adhere to manifest requirements when waste managers are also owners or other executive officers. This is also the case for voluntary adherence to employee training requirements. These results are consistent with the relationship between firm size and access to and use of expertise.

The correlations between compliance by SQGs with the manifest requirements and the respondents' rankings of several compliance constraints also reflect the limitations faced by waste managers in smaller firms. As shown in Table 5.8, respondents who ranked access to information, regulatory complexity and inflexibility, and lack of time as significant constraints on compliance were also less likely to comply. There are significant negative correlations between firm size and respondents' rankings of access to information (Kendall's tau-b coefficient $= -0.14$, $p = 0.06$) and lack of time (Kendall's tau-b coefficient $= -0.15$, $p = 0.03$) as constraints on compliance. These indicate that respondents from smaller firms rated these factors as more significant constraints on compliance.

For contingency plan compliance, the relationship between compliance and the job description of the respondent is opposite that for compliance with manifest requirements. Firms are more likely to have hazardous waste accident contingency plans when the waste manager is also the owner or other executive officer. Workplace accidents may be a greater concern to owners and executive officers than to other managers in small businesses. Owners and other executive officers who are responsible for hazardous waste management may be more concerned, therefore, with the accident implications of hazardous waste generation and management. If this is the case, it suggests that contingency plan compliance may be determined by factors largely independent of regulatory requirements.

The importance of firm profitability is mixed. The data presented in Table 5.9 suggest that the financial condition of a firm is a constraint on the development and implementation of employee training programs by VSQGs, in the absence of regulatory requirements. The results of analyzing the employee training multivariate models indicate that financial condition may be a constraint on SQG compliance as well. The financial condition of the firm is evidently not a significant constraint, however, on voluntary adherence to or compliance with the manifest or contingency plan requirements. This difference is plausible for contingency plan requirements. The annual cost of developing and implementing a training program for hazardous waste management employees is much greater than the cost of developing and maintaining a contingency plan.

The Role of Liability Knowledge

Limited knowledge of hazardous waste liability was anticipated to result in lower levels of regulatory compliance by SQGs and lower levels of voluntary adherence by VSQGs. The correlations in Table 5.9 provide evidence of such a relationship between liability knowledge and voluntary adherence by VSQGs to manifest use requirements. The multivariate compliance analyses offer further evidence of the role of liability knowledge in SQG waste management behavior.

The composite liability knowledge variable is significant and positive in both specifications of the contingency plan compliance model and in the employee training compliance model 2. There is also a significant bivariate correlation between manifest use compliance and the composite measure of liability knowledge (Kendall's tau-b coefficient = 0.32; probability value = 0.01). However, none of the manifest use compliance models employing the composite liability knowledge measure is significant at the 0.05 level; hence their exclusion from Table 5.10.[3] The individual measure of liability knowledge for transporter actions is significant in the manifest compliance models.

Ambiguous causal direction is a concern for these relationships because the data are cross-sectional. The knowledge question responses may reflect experience subsequent to decisions to comply with or voluntarily adhere to the regulations. Thus respondents may be more familiar with hazardous waste liability because they are in compliance rather than vice versa.

Analysis of the correlates of liability knowledge offers some assurance that reverse causal direction is not a problem. Liability knowledge is expected to be greatest for larger firms, for those with greater access to or use of legal and environmental management expertise, and for those in better financial condition. It is also expected that liability knowledge will be less when the waste manager is the owner or other executive officer of the firm. These assumptions are supported for access to and use of expertise and firm size as shown in Table 5.12. Neither profitability nor job category is significantly correlated with any of the liability knowledge measures, however. This may be due to the intervening effect of the expertise variables.

Thus small-business waste managers who have access to legal or environmental management expertise are more likely to be aware of the liability risks associated with hazardous waste generation and management. It seems reasonable to conclude that this knowledge was probably instrumental in regulatory compliance decisions by these waste managers. These results also suggest that adherence to contingency plan and employee training requirements by both SQGs and VSQGs may primarily

Table 5.12
Kendall's Tau-b Correlations for Liability Knowledge Variables

Determinant	Liability for Transporter Actions	Liability for Facility Actions	Strict Liability	Composite Measure
Firm Size	0.24* (0.00)[a]	0.18 (0.01)[a]	0.17 (0.03)[a]	0.26 (0.00)[a]
Profitability	0.02 (0.83)	-0.12 (0.15)	-0.11 (0.24)	-0.06 (0.54)
Owner or Other Executive Officer	-0.05 (0.58)	-0.06 (0.47)	-0.12 (0.18)	-0.11 (0.21)
Access to In-House Lawyers	0.19 (0.05)[a]	0.15 (0.29)	0.08 (0.41)	0.17 (0.09)[b]
Use of In-House Lawyers	0.18 (0.05)[a]	0.14 (0.12)	0.07 (0.48)	0.16 (0.11)
Access to In-House Environmental Experts	0.12 (0.19)	0.13 (0.12)	0.08 (0.43)	0.15 (0.12)
Use of In-House Environmental Experts	0.11 (0.20)	0.15 (0.08)[b]	0.09 (0.36)	0.15 (0.10)[b]
Access to Environmental Management Consultants	0.19 (0.04)[a]	0.09 (0.30)	0.21 (0.03)[a]	0.18 (0.05)[a]
Use of Environmental Management Consultants	0.18 (0.04)[a]	0.10 (0.23)	0.22 (0.02)[a]	0.19 (0.04)[a]

*Coefficient probability values are in parentheses.

[a]Significant at 0.05 level.
[b]Significant at 0.10 level.

be a function of good professional practice, and hence, largely determined by access to and use of expertise in waste management decisionmaking.

The Role of Regulatory Knowledge

It was also anticipated that limited knowledge of pertinent hazardous waste regulations would be a constraint on SQG compliance and VSQG voluntary adherence. The results are mixed, however. The regulatory knowledge variable was coded in two different ways. When coded as a "correct/incorrect" response to the regulatory knowledge question, the variable represents a measure of substantive knowledge of the regulations. When coded as a dichotomous "know/don't know" measure, the variable can be interpreted as a measure of regulatory familiarity rather than substantive knowledge. The survey results indicate that regulatory familiarity may be a factor in some aspects of regulatory compliance by SQGs.

Neither the substantive knowledge variable nor the regulatory familiarity variable is included in either of the multivariate SQG compliance models generated by the exploratory analysis. However, bivariate correlations are significant between the familiarity variable and contingency plan compliance at the 0.10 level (Kendall's tau-b coefficient = 0.18) and with manifest use compliance at the 0.05 level (Kendall's tau-b coefficient = 0.24). Thus SQG waste managers who answered "don't know" to the regulatory knowledge question were less likely to comply with these regulatory requirements.

The substantive knowledge variable is significantly correlated with voluntary adherence to the manifest use requirements, but the coefficient is negative. The regulation covered by the question governs the exemption of VSQGs from use of permitted hazardous waste disposal facilities. This suggests, therefore, that VSQG waste managers who are voluntarily adhering to the regulations may be unaware that they are exempt from regulation.

Regulatory familiarity is not significantly correlated with voluntary adherence to any of the regulatory requirements. Thus neither precise knowledge of the hazardous waste regulations nor overall familiarity with them appears to be an important constraint on voluntary adherence behavior by VSQGs. This further supports the hypothesis that expertise is the primary determinant of voluntary adherence.

Cost of Noncompliance and Compliance

Responses by SQG waste managers to survey questions concerning the calculative cost of noncompliance with hazardous waste regulations suggest that these dimensions of command-and-control regulatory sanctions have little impact on waste management decisionmaking by these firms. None of these variables is included in the two multivariate compliance models generated by the exploratory analysis. Bivariate correlations between the noncompliance cost variables and the compliance behavior measures also show no evidence of significant relationships. The lack of significant correlations between any of the compliance measures and respondents' estimates of maximum fine, legal fees, apprehension probability, and enforcement delay could, however, reflect threshold effects.

Tables 5.13 through 5.16 present the frequency distributions for these noncompliance cost factors. Eighty-seven percent of the respondents estimated the maximum civil fine for a first offense to be much lower than

Table 5.13
Frequency Distribution for Estimated Maximum Civil Fine

Estimated Fine	Frequency
none	26%
$ 5,000	36%
$10,000	25%
$25,000	8%
$50,000	4%

Table 5.14
Frequency Distribution for Estimated Legal Defense Fees

Estimated Defense Fees	Frequency
less than $1,000	2%
$1,000 - 2,999	14%
$3,000 - 4,999	22%
$5,000 - 10,000	38%
more than $10,000	25%

Table 5.15
Frequency Distribution for Estimated Enforcement Delay

Estimated Delay	Frequency
5 to 11 months	36%
12 to 24 months	57%
more than 24 months	7%

the statutory level of $25,000. Seventy-five percent estimated the legal cost of defending the firm against an allegation of violating the New Jersey hazardous waste regulations at less than $10,000. Sixty-four percent estimated the enforcement delay would be twelve months or more. Fifty-four percent estimated the apprehension probability at 5 percent or less, and 81 percent estimated it at 20 percent or less.

Table 5.16
Frequency Distribution for Estimated Apprehension Probability

Estimated Apprehension Probability	Frequency
5 percent or less	54%
6 to 20 percent	27%
21 to 50 percent	14%
more than 50 percent	5%

Respondents' estimates of apprehension probability may actually be high. A recent study by Ralph Jones and Gene Fax (1984b) for the EPA reports that only fourteen SQGs were inspected in New Jersey in 1984. With an estimated SQG population of between 1,600 and 2,100, the probability of inspection, much less apprehension, was on the order of 0.6 to 0.9 percent. National data on SQG inspections indicate that the average SQG can anticipate a regulatory inspection once every fifteen years (Katz 1988: 68).

High frequencies of nonresponse and "don't know" responses to questions concerning noncompliance cost suggest that respondents have difficulty estimating these elements of a rational compliance decisionmaking model. Six percent of the respondents did not answer any of the questions concerning apprehension probability, maximum fine, legal fees, or enforcement delay. "Don't know" responses to these questions ranged from 56 percent for maximum fine to 92 percent for enforcement delay. The "don't know" responses for apprehension probability and legal fees were 78 percent and 61 percent, respectively.

Many respondents may not conceptualize the risk of apprehension in probabilistic terms. The high "don't know" response frequencies for the other calculative cost variables suggest, however, that these costs, and the apprehension probability and enforcement delay constructs, are not highly salient for SQG hazardous waste managers. Thus they may not be considering the factors that are relied on as incentives to compliance in traditional command-and-control regulations.

The perceived administrative cost of compliance is the single measure employed to assess the perceived calculative cost of compliance by SQGs and voluntary adherence by VSQGs. Respondents were also asked to rank the importance of the cost of hazardous waste transportation, treatment, and disposal as a constraint on compliance.

The estimated compliance cost measure is positively correlated with

voluntary adherence to contingency plan and employee training requirements. The logit regression coefficients for administrative cost are also
positive and significant for the contingency plan multivariate models.
These positive correlations suggest reverse causality. According to rational compliance theory, compliance should be inversely correlated with
the perceived cost of compliance. However, because the question measures current perceptions of compliance costs, it is possible that responses
reflect experience that has resulted from compliance with or voluntary
adherence to the regulatory requirements. This suggests that firms currently not adhering to contingency plan and employee training requirements may be under-estimating the costs of doing so.

The correlations reported in Table 5.8 show no significant association
between respondents' rankings of the cost of hazardous waste transportation, treatment, and disposal as a constraint on compliance and their
actual compliance behavior. Nevertheless, Table 5.5 indicates that respondents ranked these costs as a very important constraint on compliance more frequently than any other potential constraint other than
regulatory complexity and inflexibility.

The liability concern variable is a proxy for the greater legal liability
for noncompliant hazardous waste management. Liability concern is significantly correlated with voluntary adherence to contingency plan requirements, but it is not included in either of the multivariate compliance
models. None of the bivariate correlations is significant between liability
concern and any of the compliance measures. Measurement error may be
responsible for the relative lack of significance of this variable. There
may not be a direct correlation between a firm's concern with hazardous
waste liability and the cost waste managers associate with such liability
in making hazardous waste management decisions.

Response to Different Regulatory Requirements

The survey results suggest that there may be significant differences
in how smaller generators respond to different regulatory requirements.
As shown in Table 5.17, correlations between manifest use compliance
and the contingency plan and employee training compliance measures are
not significant. This is also the case for voluntary adherence to these
regulatory requirements, as illustrated in Table 5.18. The contingency
plan and employee training compliance measures are significantly correlated, however, as are the comparable voluntary adherence measures.
It appears, therefore, that the phenomena of adherence to contingency
plan and employee training requirements by both SQGs and VSQGs are
similar behaviors involving related decisionmaking factors, while adherence to manifest requirements is a different behavioral phenomenon in
some respects.

Table 5.17
Kendall's Tau-b Correlations Between Compliance Measures

Compliance Measure

Compliance Measure	Contingency Plan	Employee Training	Manifest Use
Contingency Plan	1.00 $(0.00)^a$	0.36 $(0.00)^a$	0.05 (0.66)
Employee Training		1.00 $(0.00)^a$	0.13 (0.23)
Manifest Use			1.00 $(0.00)^a$

*Coefficient probability values are in parentheses.
[a]Significant at 0.05 level.
[b]Significant at 0.10 level.

Table 5.18
Kendall's Tau-b Correlations Between Measures of Voluntary Regulatory Adherence

Adherence Measure

Adherence Measure	Contingency Plan	Employee Training	Manifest Use
Contingency Plan	1.00^* $(0.00)^a$	0.35 $(0.00)^a$	-0.02 (0.92)
Employee Training		1.00 $(0.00)^a$	-0.09 (0.52)
Manifest Use			1.00 $(0.00)^a$

*Coefficient probability values are in parentheses.
[a]Significant at 0.05 level.
[b]Significant at 0.10 level.

Table 5.19
Compliance Frequencies for Individual Compliance Measures

Compliance Measure	Compliance by SQGs	Voluntary Adherence by VSQGs
Contingency Plan	33%	26%
Employee Training	68%	56%
Manifest Use	79%	32%

These differences are further supported by differences in compliance rates, as shown in Table 5.19. Both the SQG compliance rates and the VSQG rates of voluntary adherence vary substantially among the three compliance measures. The frequencies for the individual compliance measures are also substantially different for the SQGs compared to the VSQGs. T-tests of these differences in proportions reveal that they are statistically significant at the 0.05 level or better.

CONCLUSIONS

The New Jersey survey results suggest that lack of general familiarity with hazardous waste regulations may be a constraint on compliance by SQGs, while knowledge of the legal liability of hazardous waste generation is associated with greater levels of compliance and voluntary adherence to regulatory requirements by both SQGs and VSQGs.

Waste managers' general familiarity with hazardous waste regulations and substantive knowledge of hazardous waste liability appears to depend in part on their access to and use of legal or environmental management expertise. Access to or use of one or more sources of expertise is also significantly correlated with compliance and voluntary adherence to all three regulatory requirements. In addition, there is evidence that a firm's financial condition may be a constraint on developing employee training programs.

The survey results suggest that development and maintenance of contingency plan and employee training programs may reflect "good professional practice" rather than a greater ability to monitor, understand, and implement regulatory requirements. Concern with accidents *per se*, rather than regulatory compliance, may be the primary impetus behind the development of accident contingency plans in small businesses at which owners or other executive officers are responsible for hazardous waste management.

The survey analysis indicates that reliance on command-and-control regulations and enforcement of sanctions may have little effect on the waste management practices of SQGs in New Jersey, at least in the absence of initiatives to increase the salience of regulatory requirements and knowledge of sanction severity. The majority of SQG waste managers are evidently not considering the calculative cost of noncompliance in their waste management decisionmaking.

When SQG waste managers do have a sense of sanction certainty and severity, the perceived magnitude of these factors may be below most respondents' compliance action thresholds. There may be cause, therefore, for initiating efforts to inform waste managers of the true magnitude of fines for violating hazardous waste regulations, since 88 percent of the respondents underestimated the formal sanction by at least $15,000. More vigorous and visible enforcement is probably the only alternative that would change perceptions of sanction certainty. In the absence of any measure of what the decision thresholds of SQGs are for sanction severity and certainty, however, it is not possible to anticipate what level of enforcement will result in a shift in behavior.

Strict reliance on a command-and-control strategy is not likely to be cost-effective. It may not be overly difficult to increase awareness among SQGs of the actual maximum fine for violating the state's hazardous waste regulations. Significantly raising the real or perceived levels of apprehension probability, however, is likely to be very expensive given the large number of SQGs and their technological diversity.

The case for implementing educational and technical assistance programs, on the other hand, is well supported by this analysis, both for improving compliance rates by SQGs and for enhancing voluntary regulatory adherence by VSQGs. It has been supported by the work of others as well and has been recognized by at least some of the environmental regulatory agencies (DiMento 1986; Jones 1984; Katz 1988; Roberts and Bluhm 1981).

The New Jersey study offers no firm evidence that compliance costs are a significant constraint on compliance. While a large proportion of the respondents ranked the cost of hazardous waste transportation, treatment, and disposal as an important constraint on compliance, there are no significant correlations between those rankings and actual compliance behavior by SQGs. Businesses that are not complying with the regulations are evidently under-estimating the magnitude of the administrative cost of compliance.

The results of the New Jersey study should be applicable to other states in which SQGs and VSQGs are subject to levels of regulatory control similar to those of New Jersey. This analysis may also have implications for compliance and voluntary adherence behavior by other small businesses in other regulatory settings. This will depend on the technical and legal complexity of the regulations, the locus of pertinent decision-making within the firm, the salience of the regulatory concern to firm decision makers, enforcement levels, visibility of the regulatory agency, and outreach programs designed to alert firms to their regulatory obligations. The apparent differences between regulatory adherence to manifest requirements versus adherence to contingency plan and employee training requirements highlight the need to be cautious in applying these conclusions to other regulatory settings.

NOTES

1. t = t value; df = degrees of freedom; p = probability value of t value.

2. X^2 = Chi-square; df = degrees of freedom; p = probability value of Chi-square value.

3. The significance of logit regression models is based on the probability value for a Chi-square test of lack of fit. For a detailed discussion see SAS Institute (1986).

6

Enhancing Smaller
Generator Hazardous
Waste Management

Federal and state initiatives to enhance hazardous waste management by
smaller generators have focused on two distinct but related objectives: enhancing compliance with hazardous waste regulations and promoting
waste reduction. Federal initiatives have primarily consisted of grant programs to the states and some universities and research institutions, plus
development of educational materials and technical assistance services for
the regulated small quantity generators. State programs have included an
array of educational and technical assistance initiatives as well as financial
incentives and assistance and have tended to have a more intensive outreach component. Some of the state programs target the conditionally exempt VSQGs as well as SQGs. Others also provide services to large
quantity generators (OTA 1986: 208; Schwartz et al. 1987: 42).

This final chapter presents an overview of the programs that have been
employed by federal and state governments to enhance smaller generator
management of hazardous waste. I assess the different initiatives based
on both the theory and empirical research on small-business decisionmaking and regulatory compliance that is presented in previous chapters.
I also discuss evaluations that have been conducted of some of the programs. The chapter concludes with a discussion of the constraints on
effective use of enforcement and sanctions.

OVERVIEW OF FEDERAL AND STATE INITIATIVES

Federal and state concern with smaller generator management of hazardous waste lagged behind efforts to bring large generators and haz-

ardous waste treatment and disposal facilities into compliance with regulatory standards and procedural requirements. This is evidenced by the fact that federal regulation of SQGs did not become effective until 1986, some six years after the majority of the federal hazardous waste regulations went into effect in November 1980 (EPA 1980). It is further demonstrated by the continuing lack of emphasis on SQGs in federal and state enforcement programs. Once attention was focused on smaller generators, beginning with the Hazardous and Solid Waste Amendments of 1984 both federal and state agencies recognized that educational and technical assistance initiatives would be needed to promote compliance.

Direct federal initiatives included funding the 1985 national survey of smaller generators by the Environmental Protection Agency, creation of the EPA's toll-free RCRA telephone hotline to respond to generators' questions about compliance with federal hazardous waste regulations, and the development of programs within the EPA's Small Business Ombudsman's Office, including a telephone hotline dedicated to small-business questions about environmental regulations (Hill et al. 1984). The EPA prepared several educational documents for small quantity generators that have been used by the states in efforts to inform SQGs of their regulatory obligations and assist them in complying.[1]

The EPA has funded a number of state programs and some initiatives by nonprofit organizations through the RCRA 8001 grants program authorized under HSWA. Many of the grants to nonprofit organizations have been to develop services that would be available to smaller generators across the country. Examples include the development of a technical information clearinghouse by the Governmental Refuse Collectors and Disposal Association (GRCDA) and the development of a hazardous waste minimization manual by the Center for Hazardous Materials Research at the University of Pittsburgh (Katz 1988: 76).

State efforts to enhance hazardous waste management by smaller generators through nonregulatory programs are a recent phenomenon that largely reflects the availability of federal grant monies. At the time of a survey conducted by the Congressional Office of Technology Assessment in January 1986, only twelve states had hazardous waste technical assistance programs of any sort, and four others were actively planning such programs (OTA 1986: 199–200). A more recent survey conducted for the California Senate identified eighteen states with publicly funded smaller generator programs of varying extents: California, Connecticut, Florida, Georgia, Illinois, Kentucky, Maryland, Massachusetts, Michigan, Minnesota, New Jersey, New Mexico, New York, North Carolina, Pennsylvania, Tennessee, Washington, and Wisconsin (Schwartz et al. 1987: 42). According to EPA officials, if county and local government programs are included, there are some forty-two technical assistance programs for smaller generators operating in thirty-five states. However, only ten or twelve of these programs are well developed (Katz 1988: 76).

A number of the state initiatives since 1985 have been pilot projects that relied primarily on federal grants for support. Not all of these projects have evolved into continuing programs supported by the states. There has been a tendency for state initiatives, including the on-going programs, to reflect the emphasis of the federal grants programs.

The majority of state projects funded by the EPA under the RCRA Section 8001 grants of 1985 and 1986 emphasized smaller generator education and technical assistance (OTA 1986: 209). Most of the resources of these programs were first devoted to enhancing regulatory compliance by SQGs and secondarily to enhancing waste management practices and promoting waste reduction (OTA 1986: 205–7). Two more recent EPA grant programs for the states, funded in federal fiscal years 1988 and 1989, have emphasized waste reduction initiatives rather than enhancing compliance: the RCRA Integrated Training and Technical Assistance (RITTA) program and the Source Reduction and Recycling Technical Assistance program. Neither program explicitly targets smaller generators (EPA 1988b and 1988f).

Employee training has been a major emphasis of the RITTA program as well as a significant component of the grants the EPA made in 1988 for the creation of university hazardous substance research centers. The RITTA program, however, focuses primarily on training state agency personnel (EPA 1988b). The university research centers program is targeted at training both state agency personnel and private-sector employees who handle hazardous wastes at treatment and disposal facilities and businesses that generate wastes (EPA 1988d). There is no emphasis on training of smaller generator employees in these federally supported programs since SQGs are exempt from the employee training provisions of the federal hazardous waste regulations.

It is the state programs that have involved the greatest degree of direct outreach to and contact with smaller generators. With the exception of the RCRA and Small Business Ombudsman's toll-free telephone hotlines, most of the federal output has been educational materials mailed to smaller generators or made available to the states. The following section, therefore, examines state initiatives in greater detail.

SPECIFIC STATE INITIATIVES

State programs directed toward smaller generators have principally involved technical assistance and education programs. Some states have also developed financial assistance programs including grants, matching grants, low-interest loans, and tax exemptions to encourage smaller generators to invest in more advanced hazardous waste management technology, including waste reduction and onsite recycling. Several states have launched programs to reduce the cost of proper hazardous waste management by SQGs through such initiatives as waste collection route service and the establishment of transfer stations (OTA 1986: 202–3; Schecter 1987a: 7–15; Schwartz et al.: 41–70). State programs to train employees who handle hazardous wastes have primarily been limited to those funded through the RITTA grants program.

Technical Assistance and Education Programs

The principal components of state technical assistance and education programs directed toward smaller generators include the following: smaller generator identification and notification programs, direct-mail education programs associated with smaller generator identification programs, telephone hotlines for hazardous waste regulatory advice, technology transfer documents from literature reviews and applied research and pilot projects, technical information clearinghouses, onsite consultation and self-audit programs, and educational workshops for smaller generators. Employee training programs have generally not been specifically targeted at smaller generators.

Identification and Notification

Only a few states have attempted to develop comprehensive lists of regulated SQGs or businesses that may qualify as SQGs or VSQGs. Other states have relied primarily on trade associations as the means for reaching smaller generators.

New Jersey used the Standard Industrial Classification codes identified in the 1985 national survey of smaller generators conducted for the EPA to identify smaller generator industries in the state. Unemployment insurance name and address files maintained by the State Department of Labor were used to develop a mailing list of all businesses in the smaller generator SIC codes (Bozeman et al. 1986a). Minnesota has attempted to identify all regulated SQGs and have them obtain federal EPA identification numbers (Schwartz et al. 1987: 56). In 1983, Florida passed legislation requiring every county to survey its SQG population over a three-year period from 1984 through 1987 (Florida Department of Environmental Regulation 1988: 1). Counties are required to make follow-up mail contacts on an annual basis to remind SQGs of their legal responsibilities and acceptable waste management practices. Counties are also supposed to conduct updates of their surveys of SQGs every five years. In California, the State Department of Health Services works through memoranda of agreement with counties to identify SQGs and to inspect them (Russell 1985: 8).

Florida's concept of annual followups and updating of smaller generator lists is important. Because of the high rate of business starts and failures in many of the small-business industrial sectors that include smaller generators, there is considerable turnover in the population. Ready access to a state data base of businesses classified by SIC code that is regularly updated is crucial to efficient maintenance of such a contact list.

In the absence of comprehensive lists of potential smaller generators, many states and local governments have relied on trade associations as their primary means of contact. Networking through trade associations offers a number of advantages, the most important of which is establishing credibility and trust. Trade associations can also help to develop educational and technical assistance materials so that they are properly targeted to specific smaller generator audiences (Schwartz et al. 1987: 58). The major constraint on the use of trade associations as the primary conduit for contacting smaller generators is that not all smaller generator business sectors are represented by such associations (Beers 1988; Bozeman et al. 1986b: 19; Palmer et al. 1986: 87, 89). In some industrial sectors, a single trade association may serve both large and small firms. Smaller firms tend to be under-represented in the membership of these trade associations (ERM 1985: 39).

Direct Mail

Mass mailings have the advantage of reaching the largest number of firms but have significant limits to the technical detail of information that can be communicated. They are most useful for alerting smaller generators to the fact that they may generate hazardous wastes and may be subject to state and federal regulatory requirements. Mailings are of limited use in helping individual generators address specific questions about their facilities, including the applicability of specific regulations or the adoption or adaptation of specific improvements in waste management practices or advanced waste management technologies. Even simple fact sheets designed to explain the regulations and how they apply to specific SQG industrial sectors may have limited impact when a small business lacks the expertise to determine which of its byproducts constitute regulated hazardous wastes.

Telephone Hotlines

Ten of the nineteen state programs surveyed by Schwartz et al. (1987: 57) operated dedicated telephone hotlines for assisting SQGs and other generators with hazardous waste management questions. Telephone assistance includes interpreting specific regulations, determining if individual wastes are hazardous, determining how to comply with regulations, filling out manifest forms, obtaining federal EPA identification numbers, and identifying permitted hazardous waste transporters and treatment and disposal facilities. State telephone services provide an important supplement to the federal services, especially when state regulations differ from those of the federal government (Southern California Association of Governments 1985: 4–16).

Telephone assistance services are typically operated by nonregulatory state agencies or through state university extension programs (Schwartz et al. 1987: 57). The general wisdom is that inquiries will be greater when the service is not provided through a regulatory agency (OTA 1986: 211). Nevertheless, there are a number of telephone hotlines run by regulatory agencies, including those operated by the New York State Department of Environmental Conservation, the New Jersey Department of Environmental Protection, and the two federal hotlines operated by the Environmental Protection Agency. Callers can typically maintain anonymity unless a follow-up call from the technical assistance staff is required.

Telephone assistance services have the advantage of two-way communication that is not provided by printed educational materials. Major limitations include the fact that they rely on the initiative of the generator to make contact and the constraints on dealing with specific technical questions, such as waste identification, which may require onsite consultation.

Technology and Knowledge Transfer

Technology and knowledge transfer documents and information clearinghouses have limited potential for significantly affecting the waste management practices of smaller generators that do not have ready access to technical expertise (Palmer et al. 1986: 81; Steger et al. 1983: 2.7). A pilot project in Maryland demonstrated that many smaller generators need direct onsite technical assistance to benefit from available information on waste management technologies. Sloan et al. (1983: 295) summarize their findings as follows:

> The technically oriented operator, given available time, could make use of information and technology transfer services to devise a waste management strategy. The non-technical operators, who may be expert in the business and production process, may not be able to interpret technical literature effectively and may require more direct input from a technical assistance program.

Other technical assistance programs have also shown that onsite consultation may be necessary to assist smaller generators in understanding their regulatory obligations and how to comply with them (Levinson and Koskowitz 1988: 269; Nemeth and Kamperman 1986: 2–5; Russell 1985: 8; Snow 1988b: 4).

Onsite Consultation

Onsite consultation services range from informal, short-duration (one day or less) consultation at the generator's facility, to more formal onsite waste management audits, to extensive onsite waste management consultation that continues for several weeks to assist in developing and implementing changes in waste management practices or technologies.

Short-term onsite consultation typically involves addressing a very narrow compliance question, such as assisting a waste manager in determining if a given waste qualifies as a regulated hazardous waste, or helping a firm assess the adequacy of waste storage facilities and procedures.

Most onsite consultation takes the form of a more structured waste audit (Nemeth and Kamperman 1985: 10–12; Phifer and McTigue 1988: 85–86; Sloan et al. 1983: 299; Snow 1988b). A comprehensive waste management audit includes an assessment of the overall production process, as well as evaluation of individual waste streams to determine sources of substances that qualify as regulated hazardous waste. Sampling and chemical analysis may be required to make decisive waste determinations. Onsite waste management practices are also reviewed to assess compliance with regulations and opportunities for waste reduction and other cost savings.

Onsite waste audits by waste management experts have been provided free of charge or at subsidized cost by a number of states. In some cases, the state-supported audits have been targeted at representative firms to develop audit procedures for an on-going technical assistance program or self-audit checklists for direct use by other SQGs (Page and Ellsworth 1983: 303; Schwartz et al. 1987: 43; Sloan et al. 1983: 292–93). Experience has shown, however, that a certain level of waste management technical expertise is required for smaller generators to effectively use self-audits (Sloan et al. 1983: 295). One approach to confronting this constraint is to couple the self-audit guide with seminars to train personnel in using the audit procedures, followed by seminars to assist with implementation problems (Page and Ellsworth 1983: 305). The use of seminars and training workshops pose other limitations, which are discussed below.

Intensive consultation services or plant studies are more resource intensive and are strictly concerned with waste reduction and other improvements in waste management practices rather than with compliance assistance. Subsidized and free plant studies have mainly been provided through the use of engineering student interns, or over a limited period of time as part of a pilot project, such as those supported by RCRA Section 8001 grants to the states. Reports are usually produced from these studies for dissemination to other smaller generators to assist in identifying waste reduction opportunities and options.

The effectiveness of onsite consultation programs is a function of the willingness of firms to participate and their commitment to implement recommendations. In some of the pilot projects that have been undertaken, firms have been directly invited to participate. In the pilot project undertaken by the New York State Environmental Facilities Corporation (EFC), more than 90 percent of the firms contacted agreed to participate (Beers 1988). Other state onsite audit programs have relied on firms to take the initiative to request an audit following publicity of the service. No data are available to assess the level of participation under these circumstances, which typify most on-going waste audit assistance programs.

Several states have attempted to measure the effectiveness of onsite audit programs by making follow-up visits or contacts to assess the implementation of recommendations. In the EFC pilot project, very few of the conditionally exempt generators implemented waste reduction recommendations because perceived pay-back periods were too long (Beers 1988). In the Georgia Tech pilot project, 76 percent of the compliance recommendations made to the fifty firms audited were implemented (Nemeth and Kamperman 1986: 5). At the completion of the pilot project, 88 percent of the audited firms were found to be in compliance with recommendations made by the Georgia Tech auditors. In other states, scarce resources have prevented systematic followups (Cera et al. 1988: ES–4; OTA 1986: 215).

Some states, such as California and Michigan, have coupled audits with inspections by enforcement personnel (Russell 1985: 8). In such programs, smaller generators are not formally cited for regulatory violations. Deficiencies are pointed out and recommendations are made. In many cases the recommendations go beyond mere compliance and include waste reduction and cost-savings suggestions.

Seminars and Workshops

No evaluations have been done of the effectiveness of seminars and workshops in actually affecting smaller generator waste management practices. These programs have been useful in alerting businesses to their regulatory obligations, but there are no good data for measuring how effective they are in stimulating compliance or initiating advances in waste management technologies through recycling or waste reduction.

It is likely that the limitations that apply to technology transfer documents, information clearinghouses, and onsite audits also apply here: small businesses that lack in-house expertise in waste management are the least likely to benefit from such initiatives. The effectiveness of seminars and workshops is also limited by the ability and willingness of smaller generators to take the time and expense to attend. The Rockefeller Institute of Government survey found that smaller businesses are less likely to attend workshops that are more than twenty-five miles from their place of business (Palmer et al. 1986: 90–91). Factors that contribute to higher levels of participation in such workshops and seminars include co-sponsorship by trade associations; low fees or no charge for attendance; targeting specific industrial sectors; direct, personalized mailings; and involvement of local contacts (Schwartz et al. 1987: 59–60).

Financial Incentives and Assistance

States have developed financial assistance and incentive programs both to reduce the cost of compliance for smaller generators and to promote waste reduction initiatives. Initiatives to reduce compliance costs for smaller generators have primarily included state-sponsored waste collection route services and transfer stations. Financial incentive programs for waste reduction include grants for applied research and pilot projects to test waste reduction technologies. Other incentives have been provided to encourage the acquisition, installation, or construction of waste reduction or recycling equipment. These have included subsidized loans, tax-exempt revenue bonds, and other tax incentives. The EPA's Small Business Ombudsman's Office and some states also assist smaller generators in identifying financial assistance programs for which they may be eligible (EPA SBO 1984; Schecter 1987a: 10).

Initiatives to Reduce Waste Management Costs

The two primary initiatives that have been proposed to reduce the cost of compliance with hazardous waste regulations by smaller generators are the development of waste collection route services and transfer stations. Waste collection route services or "milk runs" consist of coordinated hazardous waste collection schedules among smaller generators within a defined geographic area. The objective is to reduce the unit cost of collection and transportation, which tend to be very high for smaller generators with only a few barrels of waste to ship offsite per month. As of 1987, waste collection route services for SQGs were operating in virtually every state for selected hazardous waste streams (Schwartz et al. 1987: 42). At that time, public agencies had played a role in planning some of these services, but all were operated by the private sector with no public subsidy, with the exception of the collection route service sponsored by the State of Minnesota.

The principal smaller generators served by commercial route services include dry cleaners, auto body and repair shops, and a variety of businesses and institutions that use degreasing solvents in equipment maintenance and repair or that generate photographic wastes (Beers 1988; Schwartz et al. 1987: 22). The primary wastes handled by these services include dry cleaning solvent wastes, organic degreasing solvents, paint lacquer thinner and other automotive repair wastes, and photographic wastes containing silver. Individual route service systems typically handle a single waste type or a group of compatible waste types, such as dry cleaning filter cartridges and solvent still bottoms. Relatively few services will take all of the wastes produced by smaller generators (Schwartz et al. 1987: 21).

In most cases, the state role in promoting the development of route service has included marketing assistance to route service firms and help in coordinating the development of collection routes (Schwartz et al. 1987: 65). Massachusetts has awarded a grant to a private-sector firm to study the feasibility of establishing a state route service for smaller generators (Schwartz et al. 1987: 65). Minnesota awarded a grant of $350,000 in 1985 to a private firm to develop a route service and transfer system for the full spectrum of smaller generators in the state (Cera et al. 1988: III–2–5). As of 1988, the system was limited primarily to the Twin Cities metropolitan area. Expansion of the system was anticipated, however, with the opening of a transfer facility in May 1988.

Florida has a grants program designed to encourage local governments to develop hazardous waste collection centers and route service (Campbell 1988: 5). The collection centers must provide drop-off service at least two days per year for household hazardous waste as well as for conditionally exempt VSQGs. Local governments are also required to work with hazardous waste haulers who receive contracts to service the collection centers, to develop route service for smaller generators. According to an official with the State Department of Environmental Regulation, none of the localities with grants has made any progress in developing route services (Kleman 1988). The cost of identifying customers and designing collection routes has apparently discouraged haulers from initiating such services.

The Association of Bay Area Governments (ABAG) in the San Francisco Bay area sponsored a pilot project in Alameda County, California, to coordinate VSQGs to participate in a collection route service program (Meiorin 1988: 5). California has no regulatory threshold for conditionally exempt status, so VSQGs that generate less than 100 kilograms of hazardous waste per month are subject to the same regulations as larger generators. The prime incentive for participation was the estimated reduction in disposal costs from $400 to $600 per 55-gallon drum to $200 to $300 per drum.

A previous survey of smaller generators in the ABAG region had found relatively high levels of interest in collection route service (Russell and Meiorin 1985). Actual response to the Alameda pilot project was very low, however. A total of 1,530 potential VSQGs were contacted. It was estimated that about 413 firms would qualify as VSQGs. Eighty-four businesses made an initial inquiry about the program. Only five businesses actually participated. The study found that most of the VSQGs were not using permitted hazardous waste haulers or disposal facilities and therefore were unwilling to pay the "reduced" fees available through the collection route service (Meiorin 1988: 6).

In some parts of the country, trade associations have taken the lead in coordinating their members to establish route service with a commercial firm. One example is the system established for dry cleaners in the metropolitan New York region through the Neighborhood Cleaners Association (Levinson and Koskowitz 1988: 270).

Waste Reduction Incentive Programs

Financial incentive programs targeted at waste reduction do not contribute directly to improved compliance by smaller generators. They are, therefore, only briefly discussed here.

The Rockefeller Institute of Government survey found that generators expressed greater interest in tax credits and grants for capital equipment than for any other form of financial assistance targeted at promoting waste reduction (Palmer et al. 1986: 70). Feasibility study grants and tax credits were ranked next, followed by installation loans, grants and tax credits for pilot-scale research projects, feasibility study loans, and pilot-scale research loans.

The response to financial assistance and incentive programs for waste reduction has generally been very limited by all classes of generators, with virtually no participation by smaller generators or small businesses, except in waste reduction grants programs (Cera et al. 1988: II–7; Deyle 1985: 33; Rood 1988; Schwartz et al. 1987: 45).

High transaction costs, such as the price of bond counsel to take advantage of industrial pollution control bonds, may discourage smaller businesses whose total payback from financial incentives may be relatively low (Deyle 1985: 33). In several cases, restrictions on the use of funds for capital equipment have discouraged participation (Schwartz et al. 1987: 70). Other programs have minimum project size thresholds that exclude small businesses.

The New York State Environmental Facilities Corporation (1987: 14) has recommended the creation of a revolving loan fund for smaller generators or a program to issue loan guarantees. According to the survey conducted by Schwartz et al. in 1987, only Connecticut had a loan program specifically targeted at smaller generators (Schwartz et al. 1987: 68). Staff of the Minnesota Pollution Control Agency have recommended that the state consider developing a low-interest loan fund to encourage waste reduction projects (Cera et al. 1988: II–8–9).

As of 1987, six states had grant programs that included or were targeted at smaller generator waste management (Schwartz et al. 1987: 42). Most of these are matching grant programs (Schecter 1987a: 11–15). Participation in these programs also tends to be relatively low, especially by smaller generators.

EVALUATION OF SMALLER GENERATOR PROGRAMS

Most of the state technical assistance programs have no systematic data collection or program evaluation processes (OTA 1986: 201, 215). When program evaluations are conducted, they tend to gather data only about program participants rather than the entire target population. Some have gathered data that permit the evaluation of changes in hazardous waste management by program participants (Nemeth and Kamperman 1986; Snow 1988b). Others only collect data on activity levels such as number of technical assistance phone calls handled, numbers of onsite consultations, and workshops (OTA 1986: 220).

In many cases the lack of detailed evaluations is attributed to lack of resources. It has also been suggested that states are reluctant to require information of clients because of concerns with proprietary information (OTA 1986: 215). Participation rates could be adversely affected by formal follow-up requirements.

In the absence of evaluation data on both program participants and nonparticipants, it is impossible to assess the effectiveness of state technical and financial assistance programs on explicit policy goals, such as SQG compliance or improved hazardous waste management by VSQGs. In the following sections, I offer some observations about federal and state initiatives directed at smaller generators based on the results of the New Jersey analysis and the other studies reviewed in Chapter 5, as well as the theory and empirical research on compliance and decision-making by small businesses that is presented in Chapters 2 and 3 and Rosemary O'Leary's analysis of smaller generator liability. I also highlight important questions for which the answers remain to be determined.

Supplementing Knowledge and Expertise

The analyses conducted in the New Jersey study support the conventional wisdom that holds that limited technical and regulatory knowledge and access to expertise by smaller generators can be significant constraints on compliance with hazardous waste regulations. Knowledge and expertise limitations were also shown to be associated with lower levels of voluntary adherence to hazardous waste regulations by conditionally exempt generators in the New Jersey study.

The questions that remain to be answered concern what approaches are likely to be most effective in supplementing regulatory and technical knowledge of waste managers and increasing their access to expertise. While no controlled experiments have been done, experience with various technical assistance programs indicates that two-way communication is most effective in solving specific regulatory problems and in conveying regulatory and technical information. Onsite consultations appear to be most effective, but they are also the most resource intensive and the most intrusive. Smaller generators that are distrustful of public agencies, regardless of whether they are enforcement agencies, will be least likely to participate in onsite consultation programs. Businesses concerned about what they regard as proprietary information about production processes will also be reluctant to participate in such programs.

An important question that deserves attention is how smaller generators that participate in onsite consultation programs, seminars, and workshops, and use telephone hotlines differ from those that do not. Are participants already more highly motivated to comply? Are their waste managers already more knowledgeable of the legal and technical dimensions of hazardous waste management? Do the participants' firms face fewer time, personnel, and financial constraints to compliance than nonparticipants? It may be that the smaller generators whose waste management practices pose the greatest potential threat to public health and environmental quality are also those that are least likely to participate in state-sponsored technical assistance programs.

The Role of Liability

Rosemary O'Leary's analysis of the liability risk facing both regulated SQGs and conditionally exempt VSQGs for the cleanup of hazardous waste sites makes it clear that liability is a real, if uncertain cost of hazardous waste production by smaller generators. Anecdotal evidence indicates that some SQGs and VSQGs are taking liability risk into account in their hazardous waste management decisions (Deyle 1985: 21; Katz 1988: 68). Studies of small-business decisionmaking, however, suggest that decision makers tend to ignore or discount future cost more than larger firms because of greater concern with immediate management problems, including survival, and a tendency to be reactive rather than proactive (Deeks 1976: 205; Robinson and Pearce 1984: 129; Schwartz et al. 1987: 19).

The New Jersey survey analysis indicates that waste managers' knowledge of clean-up liability is associated with compliance by SQGs and voluntary adherence to hazardous waste regulations by VSQGs. The study also indicates a correlation between liability knowledge of waste managers and their access to and use of legal and environmental management expertise.

Potential liability costs have been addressed in some information and education programs developed by the states for smaller generators. Liability is not explicitly addressed in the major federal information documents, however (EPA 1985; EPA 1986a). The magnitude of the effect of liability knowledge on hazardous waste management decisions by smaller generators remains to be determined. It appears, however, that liability knowledge can have some effect, and the cost of including it in educational and information programs is minimal.

Financial Assistance as an Incentive for Compliance

The evidence on the importance of compliance costs as a constraint on compliance by SQGs and voluntary adherence to regulations by VSQGs is mixed. The New Jersey survey revealed that smaller generators rate the cost of transportation, treatment, and disposal of hazardous wastes as a significant constraint on compliance. Yet there were no significant correlations between how respondents rated that constraint and their actual compliance behavior. The New Jersey survey did indicate, however, that the financial condition of a smaller generator is related to adherence to the state regulations requiring implementation of employee training programs.

Several qualitative analyses have concluded that transportation, treatment, and disposal costs are not a major constraint on compliance (Levinson and Koskowitz 1988: 271; Snow 1988b: 4). Both of these assessments were based, however, on information from smaller generators that voluntarily participated in onsite audit programs, workshops, and seminars. The results of the ABAG pilot project in Alameda County, California, suggest that the cost of transportation, treatment, and disposal is a significant constraint on compliance, at least by VSQGs in California. The

ABAG study concludes that collection route service will not enhance compliance when enforcement is inadequate (Meiorin 1988: 7).

As with the technical assistance programs that have been conducted by the states, there have been no formal evaluations of the impact of financial assistance initiatives on compliance. The Minnesota statewide collection service project may present such an opportunity if it is possible to assess the extent to which participants formerly did not comply with hazardous waste regulations governing the use of permitted transporters and treatment and disposal facilities.

Waste Reduction

The increasing emphasis on waste reduction in assistance programs for smaller generators reflects the expanding consensus among federal and state regulators that public resources directed toward hazardous waste management should be based on a hierarchy of integrated waste management methods (EPA 1986b: 5; EPA 1988a). This hierarchy places greatest priority on efforts to achieve waste reduction, thus limiting the amount of hazardous wastes produced that then must be managed. The second level of the hierarchy is waste recycling, followed by treatment (including incineration). Land disposal is the lowest priority waste management method. Its use should ideally be limited to disposal of residuals that cannot be otherwise dealt with at a higher level in the hierarchy.

The concept of the integrated waste management hierarchy presupposes compliance by regulated generators with the minimum standards set in federal hazardous waste regulations. The greatest threat posed by hazardous wastes is when those wastes are not managed in conformance with the standards and procedures specified in federal and state regulations. The shift in federal emphasis to waste reduction implies that the compliance problem has been dealt with adequately. One may argue this point; in fact, there has been considerable criticism of the EPA's own enforcement record as well as that of the states (GAO 1988).

An issue that has not been explicitly addressed by most federal and state programs is the cost-effectiveness of devoting public resources toward increased waste reduction by smaller generators. The argument for regulating smaller generators emphasizes the greater likelihood of waste mismanagement by smaller business. Expending public resources on regulation and compliance assistance is thus justified despite the fact that smaller generators account for less than 1 percent of all the hazardous waste produced in the country. The significance of smaller generator wastes as a threat to public health and the environment is much less in the context of the integrated waste management hierarchy. Once most smaller generators are in compliance, the greatest reductions in risk from hazardous waste management will be primarily a function of the degree of hazard of particular waste types and the volume of wastes managed. The low volumes of wastes produced by smaller generators do not offer the potential for substantial reductions in public risk through waste reduction initiatives. Waste reduction opportunities for small businesses are also often constrained by high unit costs. (Cera et al. 1988: ES–3).

The State of Minnesota has recently initiated a shift in its waste reduction technical assistance programs toward greater emphasis on medium-sized businesses (Cera et al. 1988: I–12). Experience with the state's waste reduction program indicates that technical expertise is also a constraint on waste reduction in middle-sized firms. There may be greater opportunities in middle-sized firms, however, for cost-effective investments in waste reduction that also have a more significant impact on the total volume of hazardous waste being produced (Cera et al. 1988: ES–3).

ENFORCEMENT AND SANCTIONS

A study of the options for managing hazardous wastes produced by smaller generators that was prepared for the California Senate in 1987 recommended increased enforcement to counter perceptions that authorities were not concerned with smaller generator waste management practices (Schwartz et al. 1987: 3–4). It was recommended that the state contract with county agencies to conduct inspections and that stiff penalties be imposed for violations. These recommendations are consistent with the results of the collection route service pilot project in Alameda County, California. In that study, researchers concluded that lack of enforcement resulted in little incentive for smaller generators to utilize the route service because they were avoiding the high cost of proper hazardous waste transportation and treatment altogether (Meiorin 1988: 7).

The New Jersey survey indicates that legal sanctions for noncompliance and apprehension probabilities may not even be considered by many waste managers in smaller generator firms when making decisions about waste disposal. Many respondents indicated that they did not know what the sanctions were or what the probability of apprehension or likely enforcement delays would be. The majority of those who did estimate these calculative costs of noncompliance under-estimated the formal sanctions by at least $15,000 and estimated the probability of apprehension at less than 5 percent. These results lend some credence to the argument that increased enforcement may increase compliance. They also suggest that smaller generators need to be educated about the formal sanctions they may face if apprehended.

The compliance literature suggests, however, that an important question remains to be answered before effective enforcement can take place. As discussed in Chapter 3, studies of compliance behavior indicate that decision makers have thresholds for both sanction severity and certainty. When the probability of apprehension is below their certainty threshold or the probable fine is below their severity threshold, individuals are not likely to account for these noncompliance cost factors in their decision-making. The question that remains to be answered is the following: What are these thresholds for most regulated smaller generators?

It may be that educating smaller generators about actual civil and criminal fines for noncompliance could impact their waste management behavior, if the severity of formal sanctions is above their severity thresholds. The compliance literature is fairly conclusive, however, on the greater impact of sanction certainty than sanction severity on compliance decisions (Jacob 1980: 71; Nagin 1978: 96, 110–11; Tittle 1980: 7–8). Current annual inspection probabilities are in the range of 1 percent or less. Apprehension probabilities are somewhat lower. It is clear that some effort must be made to raise the perceived probability of apprehension. Additional analysis is required, however, to determine what level of enforcement will produce a desired level of compliance.

The corporate compliance literature provides some evidence that perceived legitimacy of regulations can affect compliance levels. Federal and state educational and technical assistance programs can address this dimension of compliance decisionmaking by explaining the importance of proper hazardous waste management and the rationale behind the regulations and their application to smaller generators.

Studies of corporate compliance also suggest that smaller businesses may be sensitive to such informal sanctions as being labeled a "bad actor" by regulatory agencies, or tarnishing their public image. Regulatory agencies might advantageously use this sensitivity by publicizing significant enforcement cases and by articulating a policy of more closely monitoring the performance of firms that are flagrant violators of all environmental regulations. Such a strategy is not appropriate, however, when noncompliance results from lack of understanding of the regulations or other technical or expertise constraints. Most state enforcement agencies actively facilitate compliance rather than pursuing a rigid enforcement policy, except in cases of recalcitrance.

CONCLUSIONS

The results of the empirical studies discussed in the preceding chapter suggest that regulatory compliance by SQGs can be enhanced by increasing the knowledge waste managers have of regulations and liability and by increasing their access to and use of legal and technical expertise.

Evidently voluntary adherence by VSQGs to hazardous waste regulations can also be enhanced by increasing waste managers' knowledge of liability and by increasing their access to and use of legal and environmental management expertise.

We do not have a firm basis for judging the extent to which the cost of compliance acts as a disincentive to compliance by smaller generators or voluntary adherence to the regulations by conditionally exempt VSQGs. The New Jersey survey does indicate, however, that the financial condition of a smaller generator may be related to the likelihood that it will implement a training program for employees who handle hazardous wastes.

We have little evidence concerning the effectiveness of educational, technical, and financial assistance programs that have been implemented to date because of a general lack of formal evaluations that measure pertinent outcomes and compare behavior of participating firms with nonparticipants. No programs have been specifically targeted at promoting employee training in smaller generator businesses. Most financial assistance programs are targeted at waste reduction initiatives rather than reducing the cost of compliance. There has also been a shift in the emphasis of both federal and state technical assistance programs away from compliance assistance. Resources are being funneled primarily into waste reduction programs. There has not been an explicit assessment of the cost-effectiveness of devoting public resources to promoting waste reduction by smaller generators rather than concentrating on compliance assistance. One state, however, has redirected its waste reduction efforts toward medium-sized firms rather than smaller generators.

It is evident that many of the regulated SQGs need to be better educated about their regulatory responsibilities and the sanctions they may face for failure to comply. We do not know for certain, however, if decision makers in SQG firms have explicit thresholds for sanction severity or certainty and if so, what the range of thresholds is.

The prospects for encouraging a significant number of conditionally exempt VSQGs to voluntarily use the manifest system and permitted hazardous waste disposal facilities does not appear altogether promising. The analysis of voluntary adherence to New Jersey regulations by VSQGs estimated that only 1 to 2 percent were using the manifest system (Bozeman et al. 1986a: 119). One option that has been followed by several states is to lower the conditional exemption threshold to something less than 100 kilograms per month or eliminate it altogether. However, the size of the VSQG population may militate against extending regulatory control: 350,000 VSQGs nationally versus about 90,000 SQGs. The federal government has opted instead to upgrade the design and operational standards of sanitary landfills and other facilities that are intended to manage nonhazardous wastes but currently handle small quantities of hazardous wastes from conditionally exempt generators (EPA 1988g). This may be the more cost-effective regulatory option. It may also be more cost-effective than relying on voluntary adherence to hazardous waste regulations by VSQGs and attempting to promote such behavior through extensive public-financed educational and technical assistance programs.

Active efforts to identify potential SQGs and VSQGs not currently in state manifest system regulatory programs are essential to the effectiveness of both regulatory enforcement and educational and technical assistance initiatives. Experience in a number of states has demonstrated that many firms that qualify as SQGs or VSQGs are unaware that they generate hazardous wastes or, in the case of SQGs, that there are regulations that apply to them. There is reason, however, to question the effectiveness of relying solely on trade associations as the conduit for reaching smaller generators. Access to or development of a comprehensive listing of businesses by SIC code that is updated regularly is essential to an on-going identification and contact program.

The relatively rapid turnover of businesses within the smaller generator population implies that the federal government and the states must make long-term commitments to programs to enhance compliance. The level of resources required should level off once the current population has been effectively brought into compliance. It may not be appropriate, however, to devote the majority of federal financial assistance for the states to waste reduction until satisfactory compliance levels are achieved for smaller generators.

NOTE

1. Two EPA educational documents that have been used extensively include *Understanding the Small Quantity Generator Hazardous Waste Rules: A Handbook for Small Business* (United States Environmental Protection Agency 1986a) and *Does Your Business Produce Hazardous Wastes? Many Small Businesses Do* (United States Environmental Protection Agency 1985).

APPENDIX A

Survey Administration and Analysis

This section presents detailed information concerning the design and administration of the survey of smaller generators in New Jersey and the analysis of survey responses. Administration of the survey consisted of two major steps: a pretest and the final survey. The pretest was conducted to assess overall response rates, response bias, and effectiveness of individual questions. Copies of the final surveys administered to the manifest and nonmanifest subsamples are reproduced in Appendixes B and C.

SURVEY DESIGN

A cross-sectional mail survey was employed in this study for three reasons: because the contracting agency, the New Jersey Hazardous Waste Facilities Siting Commission, desired descriptive data on SQGs and VSQGs currently not in the state manifest system; to enable measurement of decision makers' perceptions of the costs of compliance and noncompliance and collection of information on decision maker characteristics such as knowledge and expertise; and because of the absence of any usable officical compliance data base. The enforcement data available from the New Jersey Department of Environmental Protection at the time of the study consisted entirely of manual files maintained in several regional offices. These data only covered detected cases of regulatory noncompliance. They provided no information on firms that were complying with the regulations and no data on the conditionally exempt VSQGs.

SAMPLE SELECTION

Samples for the pretest and the full survey were created by random selection from two data bases: unemployment insurance name and address files from the New Jersey Department of Labor (DOL) for the first quarter of 1985, and manifest data files from the New Jersey Department of Environmental Protection for 1983 through 1985.

Telephone calls were made to identify the appropriate contact person at each establishment and to verify mailing addresses. Firms from the DOL data base were asked if they had an EPA identification number to screen out firms that were already in the state manifest system.

The sample for analysis of SQG compliance and VSQG voluntary adherence was limited to those respondents from the DOL data base who indicated in the survey that their firms generate one or more regulated hazardous wastes. A question was asked to determine the maximum amount of hazardous waste the firm generated in a single calendar month during the preceding year. On this basis, firms were classified as SQGs if they generated a maximum of between 100 and 1,000 kilograms in any calendar month, and VSQGs if they generated less than 100 kg.

The waste generating status of respondents from the manifest data base was determined from their generating records for 1983 through November 1985. Only generators that remained below the 100 kg per month threshold for the entire three-year period were classified as VSQGs. Any generator that manifested more than 1,000 kg for one or more months during the three-year period was classified as a large quantity generator. Thus SQGs consisted of establishments that consistently generated less than 1,000 kg per month and generated 100 or more kg in at least one month of the three-year period.

THE PRETEST

The pretest was conducted in a two-wave procedure on a total sample of 200 subjects: 60 SQGs from the manifest data base and 140 establishments from the large population of probable VSQGs and SQGs outside the regulatory system. The pretest sample included only SQGs within the manifest system because the total number of VSQGs in the system was so small.

Personalized alert letters were sent to contact people to inform them about the nature of the study and to notify them that they would be receiving the questionnaire within the next few days. The second mailing consisted of the survey questionnaire and a personalized cover letter. Two and a half weeks after mailing the survey, a reminder letter was mailed to subjects who had not yet responded, along with a second copy of the survey.

Two weeks after mailing the second-wave reminder, telephone calls were made to forty-three of the subjects who had not yet responded. The overall response rate for the pretest was 17 percent. The telephone calls to nonrespondents indicated that questionnaire length was largely responsible for the low response rate. The final survey was shortened, therefore, by about 25 percent.

The follow-up calls also revealed that nearly 20 percent of the nonrespondents felt the survey did not apply to them because they did not think they generated hazardous wastes. Although the pretest was designed to filter out respondents whose organizations were not hazardous waste generators, data were also sought to characterize those firms. The final survey was altered to filter out nongenerators with the third question. The cover sheet to the survey and the accompanying cover letter specifically requested subjects to complete the first three questions at a minimum, even if they believed that their organizations did not generate hazardous waste.

The follow-up telephone calls also demonstrated that telephone contact with nonrespondents could substantially increase the survey response rate, particularly when nonrespondents had never received the survey or when they did not unnderstand some of the questions or felt the survey did not apply to them. A telephone contact step was added, therefore, between the second and third waves of the administration protocol for the final survey.

A response bias analysis was conducted to determine if there was any significant bias resulting from the time at which subjects responded. Correlations were calculated between each of the response questions and the date and wave of response. No correlations that indicated any significant bias problem were found. Some questions were rescaled to enhance response variability and others that illicited no significant variation were dropped from the final survey.

SURVEY ADMINISTRATION

Administration of the final survey followed a process that incorporated three additional steps beyond those employed in the pretest: an interim-wave mailing, telephone contacts with nonrespondents before the third-wave mailing, and verification telephone calls to a subsample of respondents after the third-wave mailing.

When nonrespondents indicated during the follow-up calls that they were having difficulty with the questions, one of the technical staff assisted them with the questions. In most instances, this led to surveys being completed by the subject. In fewer than ten cases, surveys were completed over the phone by the technical staff person.

Two weeks after the third-wave mailing, telephone calls were made to thirty respondents from the sample of establishments not currently in the manifest system to verify responses concerning waste generation. Calls were made only to respondents who had indicated that their organization did not generate any wastes in the eight categories included in the survey:

1. aqueous wastes
2. halogenated solvents
3. nonhalogenated solvents
4. waste oils
5. other combustible liquids
6. other noncombustible liquids
7. organic sludges and solids
8. inorganic sludges and solids

The total number of usable questionnaires for the final survey was 414, yielding a response rate of 41.4 percent. One establishment surveyed as part of the sample of organizations not in the manifest system subsequently proved to be in the system. The data obtained for that firm were moved to the manifest data file. Thus the total sample sizes were 699 from the nonmanifest subpopulation and 301 from the manifest subpopulation.

RESPONSE BIAS ANALYSIS

The response bias analysis for the final survey included an analysis of time-of-response bias and an analysis of differences between the respondent samples and the two subpopulations based on firm size and industry group. Correlation coefficients were calculated for the two measures of response time (wave and date) and responses to all of the survey questions. As in the pretest, no significant bias was detected.

The analysis of sample bias involved comparing establishment sizes, measured as number of employees, and industry categories of respondents with the size and industry category distributions of the two subpopulations surveyed. Several of the industry groups were combined for

Table A.1
Comparison of Nonmanifest Subsample Respondents with Subpopulation by Industry Group

Industry Group	Respondents	Subpopulation
Pesticide Application Services; Chemical Manufacturing; Wood Preserving; Formulators; Laundries; Other Services; Photography	23%	10%
Vehicle Maintenance & Equipment Repair	29%	31%
Metal Manufacturing	23%	10%
Construction; Motor Freight Terminals; Furniture/Wood Manufacturing & Refinishing; Printing/ Ceramics; Cleaning Agents & Cosmetics Manufacturers	15%	16%
Other Manufacturing; Analytic & Clinical Laboratories; Educational & Vocational Shops; Wholesale & Retail Trades	11%	11%
Secondary SIC Codes	14%	20%

the Chi-square analysis because of small cell sizes in the original grouping. The Chi-square test of independence for the recoded industry group variable for the nonmanifest subsample indicates a significant difference between the respondents and the subpopulation ($X^2 = 55.193$, df = 5, $p = 0.00$). Table A.1 is a contingency table for this relationship with percentages for each cell.

As shown in Table A.2,, the mean and median firm sizes of the nonmanifest respondents appear to be larger than those of the subpopulation sampled. A t-test of the means for these two groups indicates, however, that they are not significantly different ($t = 0.8229$, df = 289, $p = 0.41$). Furthermore, the 95 percent confidence interval for the respondent median is 9 plus or minus 16.89. The subpopulation median, which is 4,

Table A.2
Comparison of Nonmanifest Subsample Respondents and Subpopulation for Total Employment

Size Measure	Respondents	Subpopulation
Mean	34	27
Median	9	4

occurs within this interval. Survey respondents are representative, therefore, of the nonmanifest population in terms of firm size, but the distribution of respondents among the different industry groups is not the same as that for the non manifest population.

Parallel analyses of respondents from the manifest sample compared to the manifest subpopulation indicate there may also be some sample bias. A contingency table for the relationship between the respondents and the subpopulation in terms of industry group is presented in Table A.3. The Chi-square test results indicate a significant difference between the respondents and subpopulation: $X^2 = 11.466$, df = 5, p = 0.04. T-tests of the firm size means and medians for respondents and the subpopulation also indicate a significant difference: means (t = -4.2704, df = 163, p = 0.00); medians (t = -2.4046, df = 121, p = 0.02). As shown in Table A.4, the mean and median firm sizes of the respondents are considerably smaller than those of the subpopulation sampled.

ANALYTIC METHODS FOR THE FINAL SURVEY

This section describes the bivariate and multivariate analytic techniques used to test compliance behavior by SQGs and voluntary adherence to the regulations by VSQGs. Bivariate analyses were also employed to test associations between variables that were anticipated to affect compliance or voluntary adherence behavior, such as the relationships between respondent knowledge and the respondent's access to legal or environmental management expertise.

Bivariate Analyses

Kendall's tau-b correlations were used to assess the significance of bivariate relationships in the survey analysis. This rank order correlation coefficient was used rather than Pearson's r because all of the variables were ordinally or nominally scaled.

Table A.3
Comparison of Manifest Subsample Respondents and Subpopulation by Industry Group

Industry Group	Respondents	Subpopulation
Pesticide Application Services; Chemical Manufacturing; Wood Preserving; Formulators; Laundries; Other Services; Photography	10%	15%
Vehicle Maintenance & Equipment Repair	54%	38%
Metal Manufacturing	20%	25%
Construction; Motor Freight Terminals; Furniture/Wood Manufacturing & Refinishing; Printing/ Ceramics; Cleaning Agents & Cosmetics Manufacturers	5%	7%
Other Manufacturing; Analytic & Clinical Laboratories; Educational & Vocational Shops; Wholesale & Retail Trades	8%	11%
Secondary SIC Codes	3%	4%

Table A.4
Comparison of Manifest Subsample Respondents and Subpopulation for Total Employment

Size Measure	Respondents	Subpopulation
Mean	70	164
Median	20	34

Bivariate analyses are limited to analyzing relationships between pairs of variables with no account made for the influences of other variables. When real relationships are in part controlled by other factors, the results of simple bivariate analyses can be misleading. They may under-estimate or over-estimate the effects of one variable on another. Nonetheless, bivariate analyses do provide useful indications of the general trends of relationships between variables of interest and possible influencing factors.

Bivariate analyses are also less affected than multivariate analyses by low numbers of observations. In multivariate analytic programs, the number of observations for the model is controlled by the lowest number of observations for any single variable in the model. Thus if the response rate is extremely low for one variable, as was the case for several variables in this study, the number of observations for the whole model is similarly reduced.

Multivariate Analyses

Because the dependent variables to be tested in the multivariate compliance models are all dichotomous binary choice variables, logit analysis was employed to test the linear models rather than ordinary least squares regression.[1] Interpreting the impact of a change in a given independent variable on the probability that the dependent variable will be 1 or 0 is not straightforward with logit regression because of its nonlinearity. The sign of the regression coefficient for an independent variable does determine the direction of the effect, and the magnitude of the effect increases as the size of the coefficient increases (Aldrich and Nelson 1984: 43–44). For any given independent variable, the impact of changes in that variable on the probability of the dependent variable being 1 or 0 will be greatest for changes near the midpoint of the distribution for the independent variable and least for changes near the endpoints of the distribution (Pindyck and Rubinfeld 1981: 289). Thus, for example, the effect of a change in firm size on the probability of compliance will be greatest for changes near the median of the distribution of firm sizes, but it will take a much larger change in firm size among very small or very large firms to produce a comparable change in the probability of compliance.

The predictive ability of the logit model can be assessed with several statistics generated by the LOGIST procedure in SAS that was used to analyze these data (SAS Institute 1986: 271–73). The R statistic is adjusted for the number of parameters in the model by subtracting a correction term based on two times the number of parameters (2p). It is analogous to an adjusted R^2 in ordinary least squares regression since it accounts for the number of parameters in the model. The value of R ranges between 0 and 1 if the 2p correction is ignored. A second measure of the predictive ability of the logit model provided by LOGIST is the Somer's D statistic. This is an index of rank correlation between predicted probabilities and observed outcomes. It is calculated by dividing the difference between the number of concordant pairs and discordant pairs by the total number of pairs not tied on the dependent variable. The D statistic is not, therefore, adjusted for the number of parameters in the model and typically increases as independent variables are added.

Nonresponse and "don't know" response problems limited the number of independent variables that could be included in the logit regression models. An exploratory analytic approach was used, therefore, to identify multivariate models with the greatest explanatory power and no more than ten independent variables. Initial theoretically based models with more than ten independent variables were tested by sequentially dropping variables for which the regression coefficient probability values were very high (much greater than 0.10) and for which there was not a significant bivariate relationship with the model dependent variable. Where the coefficient probability values were marginal, the variables were reintroduced after other variables had been dropped. The decision to retain or drop a variable from an individual exploratory model was made by comparing the results of running the model with and without the variable. When the variable had little effect on the R measure of model predictive ability and little effect on the magnitude and significance of other regression coefficients, the variable was dropped. The results of this exploratory analysis yielded the two multivariate models that are presented in Chapter 5.

NOTE

1. For discussions of the limitations of ordinary least squares in analyzing models with dichotomous dependent variables, see Aldrich and Nelson (1984: 13–14), Cox (1970: 16–17), and Pindyck and Rubinfeld (1981: 276–77).

APPENDIX B

Survey for Establishments Outside the New Jersey Manifest System

SMALL ENTERPRISE WASTE MANAGEMENT STUDY

SYRACUSE UNIVERSITY

TECHNOLOGY AND INFORMATION POLICY PROGRAM

SYRACUSE, NEW YORK

Thank you for participating in the Small Enterprise Waste Management Survey. The objective of this study is to provide an understanding of the current waste management practices of small businesses and non-profit organizations in New Jersey and to help develop programs to assist such organizations with hazardous waste management. Information from the survey will be used by the Technology and Information Policy Program (TIPP) to make recommendations to the New Jersey Hazardous Waste Facilities Siting Commission. TIPP is under strict contract requirements to maintain the confidentiality of individual survey responses. Data protection systems are being employed to prevent identification of individual respondents by the Siting Commission as well as any member of the public.

Please complete Questions 1 through 3 at a minimum. Even if you answer NO to all of Question #3, your response will still be of value to us.

The research team sincerely appreciates your effort in making this project a success. If there are any questions concerning this study, please contact TIPP. Thank you.

Technology and Information Policy Program
Syracuse University
103 College Place
Syracuse, New York 13244-4010
(315) 423-1890

PLEASE NOTE: NO POSTAGE IS NEEDED FOR RETURN MAIL.

DIRECTIONS: Check one code number for each question unless otherwise specified. Please respond to every question.

1. Check the one job description that most closely corresponds to your job duties:

    _____ a. Owner of organization

    _____ b. President, executive director, or chief executive officer of organization

    _____ c. Operations or production engineer/manager/ supervisor/foreman

    _____ d. Parent company manager or engineer

    _____ e. Other
    [describe]:_____

2. Which of the following statements below provides the most accurate description of your organization's profitability in 1985?

    _____ a. Not applicable, we are a non-profit or government organization

    _____ b. Our organization sustained severe losses

    _____ c. Our organization sustained modest losses

    _____ d. Our organization made modest profits

    _____ e. Our organization made good profits

    _____ f. Our organization made excellent profits

The next series of questions concern the waste products generated by your organization at this location.

The terms waste product or wastes, as used in this survey, include any solid, liquid, semi-solid, or contained gaseous by-product, garbage, refuse, or sludge that is produced in the performance of a service or from a manufacturing or chemical process and that is disposed of, burned, treated, or recycled. Wastes disposed of through a public sewer or septic system are considered waste products here.

For purposes of this survey, definitions of the different waste
  types are as follows:

OILS - automotive oils, industrial oils, fuel oils, and others

AQUEOUS LIQUIDS - water soluble liquid wastes including acids
  and alkalis (bases or caustics), cyanides, spent plating
  wastes, and photographic wastes,

HALOGENATED SOLVENTS - solvents containing chlorine, fluorine,
  iodine, or bromine, such as chlorobenzenes, trichloro-
  ethylene, perchloroethylene, and methylene chloride

NONHALOGENATED SOLVENTS - other solvents such as benzene,
  acetone, toluene, methanol, ethyl cellulose, and xylenes

OTHER LIQUIDS THAT ARE COMBUSTIBLE - liquids capable of being
  burned, with a flashpoint of less than $140^\circ F$ (60° C), such as
  discarded or recycled paints, varnishes, and lacquers that
  contain solvents; stripping agents; paint brush cleaners;
  epoxy resins; rubber cements; marine glues; and waste inks
  containing solvents

OTHER LIQUIDS THAT ARE NOT COMBUSTIBLE - nonflammable liquids
  with a flashpoint greater than $140^\circ F$ ($60^\circ C$) such as liquid
  paint wastes without solvents, washing and rinsing solutions
  containing pesticides or heavy metals (arsenic, barium,
  cadmium, lead, mercury, selenium, or silver), waste inks
  containing heavy metals, and waste pesticides

ORGANIC SLUDGES AND SOLIDS - sludges and solids containing
  organic wastes, including oily residues, solvent still
  bottoms (distillation residues from reclaiming spent solvents), filtration residues from dry cleaning operations, and
  wastewater treatment sludges containing pentachlorophenol or
  creosote

INORGANIC SLUDGES AND SOLIDS - dusts, sludges, and solids with
  heavy metals, sludges from ink formation, sludges from photographic processes, paint residues, pesticide containers, and
  wastewater treatment sludges containing heavy metals

3. Please indicate which of these waste types your organization produces, if any:

(a) oils

_____   _____
yes   no

(b) aqueous liquids

_____   _____
yes   no

(c) halogenated solvents

_____   _____
yes   no

(d) nonhalogenated solvents

_____   _____
yes   no

(e) other liquids that are combustible

_____   _____
yes   no

(f) other liquids that are not combustible

_____   _____
yes   no

(g) organic sludges or solids

_____   _____
yes   no

(h) inorganic sludges or solids

_____   _____
yes   no

(i) other wastes [describe]: _____

_____

_____

[If you answered NO for each of the eight specific waste types (a-h), stop here. If you answered YES for any of the specific waste types, go on to the next question.]

4. Does your organization maintain a written hazardous waste accident contingency plan that describes actions your personnel shall take in response to fires, explosions, or any unplanned release of hazardous waste to the environment?

_____ No

_____ Yes

5. Some organizations who produce wastes in these categories provide on-the-job or classroom training to employees who handle such wastes. Which of the following characteristics apply to your organization's waste handling training? [Check all that apply.]

    _____ (a) our employees do not receive any formal hazardous waste handling training

    _____ (b) our employees are taught proper methods of handling hazardous wastes and safety procedures

    _____ (c) our employees are taught emergency procedures for spills· or accidents

    _____ (d) our employees are taught how to use emergency equipment and systems

    _____ (e) our employees are taught by a person trained in hazardous waste management procedures

For the following questions, please indicate the appropriate response by placing an "X" on the line above the code that represents your level of agreement or disagreement with each statement:

SA = Strongly Agree   A = Agree   ? = Neither Agree Nor Disagree

D = Disagree   SD = Strongly Disagree

6. In our organization, potential legal liability is not one of the most significant concerns in deciding how to manage our waste products.

      SA   A   ?   D   SD

7. The costs associated with not complying with New Jersey hazardous waste regulations usually outweigh the costs of complying.

      SA   A   ?   D   SD

8. The State of New Jersey and the federal government have designated certain kinds of waste products as hazardous. Please indicate whether you think each of the following statements is true or false for organizations that generate such hazardous wastes:

	true	false	don't know/ not sure
(a) They would not be liable if their wastes were removed from their property by a second party.	___	___	___
(b) They would be liable if their wastes were delivered to a second party by themselves or by another transporter, but the liability would not extend indefinitely.	___	___	___
(c) They would not be liable if their wastes were disposed of at a treatment or disposal facility with a permit to handle hazardous wastes.	___	___	___
(d) They would be liable regardless of how their wastes were disposed, and the liability would extend indefinitely.	___	___	___
(e) Under New Jersey regulations, any organization that produces less than 220 pounds (100 kilograms) of a non-acute hazardous waste in a calendar month may legally dispose of that waste in a landfill that is permitted for dry industrial waste.	___	___	___

9. To what extent does your organization make use of the following individuals or organizations for advice on managing your waste products?

	not aware of this source	never/ not avail- able	some- times	often
(a) New Jersey Dept of Environmental Protec- tion (NJDEP) telephone hotline	___	___	___	___
(b) NJDEP publications	___	___	___	___
(c) Legal consultants	___	___	___	___
(d) In-house or parent company lawyers	___	___	___	___
(e) Environmental manage- ment or engineering consultants	___	___	___	___
(f) In-house or parent company environmental managers or engineers	___	___	___	___

For Questions 10 and 11, when reporting waste amounts, please include units using the following symbols:

P = pounds   KG = kilograms   CY = cubic yards

L = liters   T = tons   G = gallons

B = 55-gallon barrels

10. What is the maximum total amount of wastes included in the eight specific waste categories listed in Question #3 that your organ- ization has generated at this location in a single calendar month during the past year? [If none, enter 0.]

_____   _____
       amount   units

11. What is the maximum total amount of wastes included in these waste categories that your organization has stored onsite at this location for any period of 90 days or more during the past year? [**If none, enter 0.**]

_____   _____
       amount   units

12. Approximately how much did your organization spend in 1985 to transport and treat, dispose of, or recycle wastes included in these categories? [**Include any record keeping, or other administrative costs.**]

_____ less than $200   _____ $1,500 - 1,999

_____ $200 - 499   _____ $2,000 - 2,999

_____ $500 - 999   _____ $3,000 - 5,000

_____ $1,000 - 1,499   _____ more than $5,000

13. For wastes in these categories, some organizations provide information to the transporter about the content and nature of the wastes being transported. If your organization provides such information to transporters, how does it do so? [**Check all that apply.**]

_____ (a) we do not ship wastes off-site

_____ (b) no formal notice usually given

_____ (c) the containers are labelled

_____ (d) the transporter is notified verbally

_____ (e) the transporter is notifed in writing

_____ (f) New Jersey or other state or federal hazardous waste manifest form

_____ (g) New Jersey or federal Department of Transportation shipping paper

14. What proportion of the wastes in these categories that are produced by your organization at this location are treated, disposed of, or recycled at facilities with state or federal hazardous waste permits?

_____ none   _____ 75 - 99 %

_____ 1 - 24 %   _____ 100 % [skip to Question #16]

_____ 25 - 49 %   _____ don't know

_____ 50 - 74 %

15. If your organization had treated, disposed of, or recycled all (100 %) of its wastes in these categories at facilities with hazardous waste permits in 1985, how much do you estimate your organization would have spent for both transportation and for treatment, disposal, or recycling? [including administrative costs]

_____ less than $200   _____ $1,500 - 1,999

_____ $200 - 499   _____ $2,000 - 2,999

_____ $500 - 999   _____ $3,000 - 5,000

_____ $1,000 - 1,499   _____ more than $5,000

16. How much would you estimate it costs an organization similar to yours, **over the course of one year**, to complete the necessary paper work, record keeping, and other administrative tasks involved in using the New Jersey manifest system for tracking all of its shipments of hazardous waste?

_____ less than $100/year

_____ $100 - 299/year

_____ $300 - 499/year

_____ $500 - 1,000/year

_____ more than $1,000/year

_____ don't know

For Questions 17 - 18, only mark the columns for those waste types pro-
    duced by your organization (those for which you checked "yes" in
    Question 3). When reporting units, use the symbols defined for
    Questions 10 - 11.

	Aqueous Liquids		Halogenated Solvents		Nonhalogenated Solvents	
	Amount	Unit	Amount	Unit	Amount	Unit
17. What is the total amount of each waste type produced by your organization at this location in 1985? [include units]	_____	___	_____	___	_____	___

18. How much of each waste
    type produced by your
    organization was treated,
    recycled, or disposed of
    by each of the following
    means in 1985? [include
    units]

	Aqueous Liquids		Halogenated Solvents		Nonhalogenated Solvents	
(a) don't know/not sure	_____	___	_____	___	_____	___
(b) onsite* landfill	_____	___	_____	___	_____	___
(c) off-site landfill	_____	___	_____	___	_____	___
(d) onsite incinerator	_____	___	_____	___	_____	___
(e) off-site incinerator	_____	___	_____	___	_____	___
(f) burned onsite as a fuel	_____	___	_____	___	_____	___
(g) burned off-site as a fuel	_____	___	_____	___	_____	___
(h) public sewer system	_____	___	_____	___	_____	___

---

* "On-site" refers to activities that take place in the same loca-
    tion as the service or manufacturing operation that produces a
    waste product.

Oils		Other Combust- ible Liquids		Other Noncombust- ible Liquids		Organic Solids		Inorganic Solids	
Amount	Unit	Amount	Unit	Amount	Unit	Amount	Unit	Amount	Unit
——	——	——	——	——	——	——	——	——	——
——	——	——	——	——	——	——	——	——	——
——	——	——	——	——	——	——	——	——	——
——	——	——	——	——	——	——	——	——	——
——	——	——	——	——	——	——	——	——	——
——	——	——	——	——	——	——	——	——	——
——	——	——	——	——	——	——	——	——	——
——	——	——	——	——	——	——	——	——	——
——	——	——	——	——	——	——	——	——	——

	Aqueous Liquids		Halogenated Solvents		Nonhalogenated Solvents	
	Amount	Unit	Amount	Unit	Amount	Unit
(i) private septic tank/leach field system	_____	___	_____	___	_____	___
(j) treated onsite (for example, neutralized, filtered, or evaporated)	_____	___	_____	___	_____	___
(k) treated off-site	_____	___	_____	___	_____	___
(l) blended to produce a fuel	_____	___	_____	___	_____	___
(m) recycled or reused onsite	_____	___	_____	___	_____	___
(n) recycled or reused off-site (including waste exchange)	_____	___	_____	___	_____	___
(o) applied directly to the land, for example as fertilizer, soil conditioner, or dust suppressant	_____	___	_____	___	_____	___

Oils		Other Combustible Liquids		Other Noncombustible Liquids		Organic Solids		Inorganic Solids	
Amount	Unit	Amount	Unit	Amount	Unit	Amount	Unit	Amount	Unit
___	___	___	___	___	___	___	___	___	___
___	___	___	___	___	___	___	___	___	___
___	___	___	___	___	___	___	___	___	___
___	___	___	___	___	___	___	___	___	___
___	___	___	___	___	___	___	___	___	___
___	___	___	___	___	___	___	___	___	___
___	___	___	___	___	___	___	___	___	___

19. Studies have shown that enforcement delays (time between detection of a violation and enforcement action to bring compliance) vary significantly among the states for hazardous waste regulations (for example, 18 months in one state, six months in an-other, less than one month in a third). What do you estimate the delay is in New Jersey?

    _____ months

    _____ don't know

20. Last year, a private research firm estimated that 10,000 small businesses and manufacturers in New Jersey were not complying with hazardous waste regulations. What/centage of those organizations would you predict were detected and prosecuted by state regulatory officials?

    _____ percent

    _____ don't know

21. If an organization were prosecuted by the State of New Jersey for failing to file a manifest form to track the shipment of a hazardous waste, what would you estimate the maximum applicable fine to be for the first offense?

    _____ no fine   _____ $25,000

    _____ $5,000   _____ $50,000

    _____ $10,000   _____ don't know

22. If an organization were prosecuted by the State of New Jersey for failing to file a manifest form to track the shipment of a hazardous waste, how much do you estimate it would cost the organization in legal fees and other costs to defend itself in an enforcement action by the state?

    _____ less than $1,000   _____ $5,000 - 10,000

    _____ $1,000 - 2,999   _____ more than $10,000

    _____ $3,000 - 4,999   _____ don't know

23. In your organization's efforts to comply with state and federal laws and regulations that apply to waste products you may produce, how important is each of the following constraints?

	Very important constraint	Somewhat important constraint	A constraint but not important	Not a constraint for our company
(a) Complexity or inflexibility of state regulations	_____	_____	_____	_____
(b) Lack of time to stay informed of applicable regulations	_____	_____	_____	_____
(c) Technical difficulty of determining if wastes are hazardous	_____	_____	_____	_____
(d) High cost of determining if wastes are hazardous	_____	_____	_____	_____
(e) Access to hazardous waste management technology information	_____	_____	_____	_____
(f) Identifying transporters with hazardous waste permits	_____	_____	_____	_____
(g) Identifying treatment or disposal facilities with hazardous waste permits	_____	_____	_____	_____
(h) High costs of hazardous waste treatment or disposal at permitted facilities and transportation to such facilities	_____	_____	_____	_____
(i) High costs of waste management technical consultants	_____	_____	_____	_____
(j) Unavailability of hazardous waste management technical experts within our organization	_____	_____	_____	_____

THANK YOU FOR PARTICIPATING IN THIS STUDY!

APPENDIX C

Survey for Establishments Within the New Jersey Manifest System

SMALL QUANTITY GENERATOR

WASTE MANAGEMENT STUDY

SYRACUSE UNIVERSITY

TECHNOLOGY AND INFORMATION POLICY PROGRAM

SYRACUSE, NEW YORK

Thank you for participating in the Small Quantity Generator Waste Management Survey. The objective of this study is to provide an understanding of the current waste management practices of small businesses and non-profit organizations in New Jersey and to help develop programs to assist such organizations with hazardous waste management. Information from the survey will be used by the Technology and Information Policy Program (TIPP) to make recommendations to the New Jersey Hazardous Waste Facilities Siting Commission. TIPP is under strict contract requirements to maintain the confidentiality of individual survey responses. Data protection systems are being employed to prevent identification of individual respondents by the Siting Commission as well as any member of the public.

The research team sincerely appreciates your effort in making this project a success. If there are any questions concerning this study, please contact TIPP. Thank you.

Technology and Information Policy Program
Syracuse University
103 College Place
Syracuse, New York 13244-4010
(315) 423-1890

PLEASE NOTE: NO POSTAGE IS NEEDED FOR RETURN MAIL.

DIRECTIONS: Check one code number for each question unless otherwise specified. Please respond to every question.

1. Check the one job description that most closely corresponds to your job duties:

   _____ a. Owner of organization

   _____ b. President, executive director, or chief executive officer of organization

   _____ c. Operations or production engineer/manager/ supervisor/foreman

   _____ d. Parent company manager or engineer

   _____ e. Other
               [describe]:_____

2. Approximately how many people are employed at this location?

   _____ people.

3. Which of the following statements below provides the most accurate description of your organization's profitability in 1985?

   _____ a. Not applicable, we are a non-profit or government organization

   _____ b. Our organization sustained severe losses

   _____ c. Our organization sustained modest losses

   _____ d. Our organization made modest profits

   _____ e. Our organization made good profits

   _____ f. Our organization made excellent profits

4. What products or services are produced or delivered by your organization at this location (list as many as three products or services):

_____ (1)

_____ (2)

_____ (3)

The next series of questions concern the waste products generated by your organization at this location.

The terms waste product or wastes, as used in this survey, include any solid, liquid, semi-solid, or contained gaseous by-product, garbage, refuse, or sludge that is produced in the performance of a service or from a manufacturing or chemical process and that is disposed of, burned, treated, or recycled. Wastes disposed of through a public sewer or septic system are considered waste products here.

For purposes of this survey, definitions of the different waste types are as follows:

OILS - automotive oils, industrial oils, fuel oils, and others

AQUEOUS LIQUIDS - water soluble liquid wastes including acids and alkalis (bases or caustics), cyanides, spent plating wastes, and photographic wastes,

HALOGENATED SOLVENTS - solvents containing chlorine, fluorine, iodine, or bromine, such as chlorobenzenes, trichloro-ethylene, perchloroethylene, and methylene chloride

NONHALOGENATED SOLVENTS - other solvents such as benzene, acetone, toluene, methanol, ethyl cellulose, and xylenes

OTHER LIQUIDS THAT ARE COMBUSTIBLE - liquids capable of being burned, with a flashpoint of less than 140°F (60° C), such as discarded or recycled paints, varnishes, and lacquers that contain solvents; stripping agents; paint brush cleaners; epoxy resins; rubber cements; marine glues; and waste inks containing solvents

OTHER LIQUIDS THAT ARE NOT COMBUSTIBLE - nonflammable liquids with a flashpoint greater than 140°F (60°C) such as liquid paint wastes without solvents, washing and rinsing solutions containing pesticides or heavy metals (arsenic, barium, cadmium, lead, mercury, selenium, or silver), waste inks containing heavy metals, and waste pesticides

ORGANIC SLUDGES AND SOLIDS - sludges and solids containing organic wastes, including oily residues, solvent still bottoms (distillation residues from reclaiming spent solvents), filtration residues from dry cleaning operations, and wastewater treatment sludges containing pentachlorophenol or creosote

INORGANIC SLUDGES AND SOLIDS - dusts, sludges, and solids with heavy metals, sludges from ink formation, sludges from photographic processes, paint residues, pesticide containers, and wastewater treatment sludges containing heavy metals

5. Please indicate which of these waste types your organization produces, if any:

(a) oils

        yes   no

(b) aqueous liquids

        yes   no

(c) halogenated solvents

        yes   no

(d) nonhalogenated solvents

        yes   no

(e) other liquids that are combustible

        yes   no

(f) other liquids that are not combustible

        yes   no

(g) organic sludges or solids

        yes   no

(h) inorganic sludges or solids

        yes   no

(i) other wastes [describe]: _____

_____

_____

6. Does your organization maintain a written hazardous waste accident contingency plan that describes actions your personnel shall take in response to fires, explosions, or any unplanned release of hazardous waste to the environment?

   _____ No

   _____ Yes

7. Some organizations who produce wastes in these categories provide on-the-job or classroom training to employees who handle such wastes. Which of the following characteristics apply to your organization's waste handling training? **[Check all that apply.]**

   _____ (a) our employees do not receive any formal hazardous waste handling training

   _____ (b) our employees are taught proper methods of handling hazardous wastes and safety procedures

   _____ (c) our employees are taught emergency procedures for spills or accidents

   _____ (d) our employees are taught how to use emergency equipment and systems

   _____ (e) our employees are taught by a person trained in hazardous waste management procedures

For Questions 8 and 9, please indicate the appropriate response by placing an "X" on the line above the code that represents your level of agreement or disagreement with each statement:

SA = Strongly Agree   A = Agree   ? = Neither Agree Nor
                                                   Disagree

D = Disagree   SD = Strongly Disagree

8. In our organization, potential legal liability is not one of the most significant concerns in deciding how to manage our waste products.

                              SA   A   ?   D   SD

9. The costs associated with not complying with New Jersey hazardous waste regulations usually outweigh the costs of complying.

                              SA   A   ?   D   SD

10. To what extent does your organization make use of the following individuals or organizations for advice on managing your waste products?

	not aware of this source	never/ not avail- able	some- times	often
(a) New Jersey Dept of Environmental Protection (NJDEP) telephone hotline	___	___	___	___
(b) NJDEP publications	___	___	___	___
(c) Legal consultants	___	___	___	___
(d) In-house or parent company lawyers	___	___	___	___
(e) Environmental management or engineering consultants	___	___	___	___
(f) In-house or parent company environmental managers or engineers	___	___	___	___

11. The State of New Jersey and the federal government have designated certain kinds of waste products as hazardous. Please indicate whether you think each of the following statements is true or false for organizations that generate such hazardous wastes:

	true	false	don't know/ not sure
(a) They would not be liable if their wastes were removed from their property by a second party.	____	____	____
(b) They would be liable if their wastes were delivered to a second party by themselves or by another transporter, but the liability would not extend indefinitely.	____	____	____
(c) They would not be liable if their wastes were disposed of at a treatment or disposal facility with a permit to handle hazardous wastes.	____	____	____
(d) They would be liable regardless of how their wastes were disposed, and the liability would extend indefinitely.	____	____	____
(e) Under New Jersey regulations, any organization that produces less than 220 pounds (100 kilograms) of a non-acute hazardous waste in a calendar month may legally dispose of that waste in a landfill that is permitted for dry industrial waste.	____	____	____

For Questions 12 and 13, when reporting waste amounts, please include units using the following symbols:

P = pounds   KG = kilograms   CY = cubic yards

L = liters   T = tons   G = gallons

B = 55-gallon barrels

12. What is the maximum total amount of wastes included in the eight specific waste categories listed in Question #5 that your organization has generated at this location in a single calendar month during the past year? [If none, enter 0.]

_____   _____
        amount   units

13. What is the maximum total amount of wastes included in these waste categories that your organization has stored onsite at this location for any period of 90 days or more during the past year? [If none, enter 0.]

_____   _____
        amount   units

14. Approximately how much did your organization spend in 1985 to transport and treat, dispose of, or recycle wastes included in these categories? [Include any record keeping, or other administrative costs.]

_____ less than $200   _____ $1,500 - 1,999

_____ $200 - 499   _____ $2,000 - 2,999

_____ $500 - 999   _____ $3,000 - 5,000

_____ $1,000 - 1,499   _____ more than $5,000

15. For wastes in these categories, some organizations provide information to the transporter about the content and nature of the wastes being transported. If your organization provides such information to transporters, how does it do so? [Check all that apply.]

_____ (a) we do not ship wastes off-site

_____ (b) no formal notice usually given

_____ (c) the containers are labelled

_____ (d) the transporter is notified verbally

_____ (e) the transporter is notifed in writing

_____ (f) New Jersey or other state or federal hazardous waste manifest form

_____ (g) New Jersey or federal Department of Transportation shipping paper

16. What proportion of the wastes in these categories that are produced by your organization at this location are treated, disposed of, or recycled at facilities with state or federal hazardous waste permits?

_____ none   _____ 75 - 99 %

_____ 1 - 24 %   _____ 100 % [skip to Question #18]

_____ 25 - 49 %   _____ don't know

_____ 50 - 74 %

17. If your organization had treated, disposed of, or recycled all (100 %) of its wastes in these categories at facilities with hazardous waste permits in 1985, how much do you estimate your organization would have spent for both transportation and for treatment, disposal, or recycling? [including administrative costs]

_____ less than $200   _____ $1,500 - 1,999

_____ $200 - 499   _____ $2,000 - 2,999

_____ $500 - 999   _____ $3,000 - 5,000

_____ $1,000 - 1,499   _____ more than $5,000

18. How much would you estimate it costs an organization similar to yours, **over the course of one year**, to complete the necessary paper work, record keeping, and other administrative tasks involved in using the New Jersey manifest system for tracking all of its shipments of hazardous waste?

_____ less than $100/year   _____ $500 - 1,000/year

_____ $100 - 299/year   _____ more than $1,000/year

_____ $300 - 499/year   _____ don't know

19. Studies have shown that enforcement delays (time between detection of a violation and enforcement action to bring compliance) vary significantly among the states for hazardous waste regulations (for example, 18 months in one state, six months in another, less than one month in a third). What do you estimate the delay is in New Jersey?

_____ months   _____ don't know

20. Last year, a private research firm estimated that 10,000 small businesses and manufacturers in New Jersey were not complying with hazardous waste regulations. What percentage of those organizations would you predict were detected and prosecuted by state regulatory officials?

_____ percent   _____ don't know

21. If an organization were prosecuted by the State of New Jersey for failing to file a manifest form to track the shipment of a hazardous waste, what would you estimate the maximum applicable fine to be for the first offense?

_____ no fine   _____ $25,000

_____ $5,000   _____ $50,000

_____ $10,000   _____ don't know

22. If an organization were prosecuted by the State of New Jersey for failing to file a manifest form to track the shipment of a hazardous waste, how much do you estimate it would cost the organization in legal fees and other costs to defend itself in an enforcement action by the state?

_____ less than $1,000   _____ $5,000 - 10,000

_____ $1,000 - 2,999   _____ more than $10,000

_____ $3,000 - 4,999   _____ don't know

23. In your organization's efforts to comply with state and federal laws and regulations that apply to waste products you may produce, how important is each of the following constraints?

	Very important constraint	Somewhat important constraint	A constraint but not important	Not a constraint for our company
(a) Complexity or inflexibility of state regulations	____	____	____	____
(b) Lack of time to stay informed of applicable regulations	____	____	____	____
(c) Technical difficulty of determining if wastes are hazardous	____	____	____	____
(d) High cost of determining if wastes are hazardous	____	____	____	____
(e) Access to hazardous waste management technology information	____	____	____	____
(f) Identifying transporters with hazardous waste permits	____	____	____	____
(g) Identifying treatment or disposal facilities with hazardous waste permits	____	____	____	____
(h) High costs of hazardous waste treatment or disposal at permitted facilities and transportation to such facilities	____	____	____	____
(i) High costs of waste management technical consultants	____	____	____	____
(j) Unavailability of hazardous waste management technical experts within our organization	____	____	____	____

THANK YOU FOR PARTICIPATING IN THIS STUDY!

Bibliography

Abt Associates, Inc. 1983. *Final Recommendations on Inclusion/Exclusion of Industries by SIC Code for Small Quantity Generator Survey.* Cambridge, Mass.

Acton Society Trust. 1956. *Management Succession.* London.

Aldrich, John H. and Forrest D. Nelson. 1984. *Linear Probability, Logit and Probit Models.* Beverly Hills, Calif.: Sage Publications.

Allison, Graham T. 1971. *Essence of Decision Explaining the Cuban Missile Crisis.* Boston: Little, Brown & Company.

American Institute of Certified Public Accountants [AICPA]. 1983. *Underreported Taxable Income.* Washington, D.C.

Anderson, Frederick A., Allen V. Kneese, Phillip D. Reed, Russell B. Stevenson and Serge Taylor. 1977. *Environmental Improvement Through Economic Incentives.* Baltimore: Johns Hopkins Press.

Anonymous. 1979. "Developments in the Law—Corporate Crime: Regulating Corporate Behavior through Criminal Sanctions." *Harvard Law Review* 92: 1227–375.

Aranson, Peter H. 1982. "Pollution Control: The Case for Competition." In *Instead of Regulation,* Robert W. Poole, ed. Lexington, Mass.: Lexington Books.

Bain, Joe S. 1973. *Environmental Decay: Economic Causes and Remedies.* Boston: Little, Brown & Company.

Bardach, Eugene and Robert A. Kagan. 1982. "Liability Law and Social Regulation." In *Social Regulation: Strategies for Reform,* Eugene Bardach and Robert A. Kagan, eds. San Francisco: Institute for Contemporary Studies.

Baumol, William J. 1972. "On Taxation and the Control of Externalities." *American Economic Review* 62 (June): 307–322.

Becker, Gary S. 1974. "Crime and Punishment: An Economic Approach." In *Essays in the Economics of Crime and Punishment*, Gary S. Becker and William M. Landes, eds. New York: Columbia University Press.

Beers, Andy. New York State Legislative Commission on Toxic Substances and Hazardous Wastes. 1988. Personal communication, November 28.

Boraiko, Allen A. 1985. "Storing Up Trouble... Hazardous Waste," *National Geographic*, 167 (3): 318–51.

Bozeman, Barry L., Robert E. Deyle, Rosemary O'Leary, and Philip D. Schuller. 1986a. *New Jersey Small Quantity Generator Survey and Analysis. Volume I: Extrapolation from National Survey and Compliance Analysis.* Trenton: New Jersey Hazardous Waste Facilities Siting Commission.

Bozeman, Barry L., Robert E. Deyle, and Rosemary O'Leary. 1986b. *New Jersey Small Quantity Generator Survey and Analysis. Volume IV: Survey of New Jersey Small Quantity Generators.* Trenton: New Jersey Hazardous Waste Facilities Siting Commission.

Braithwaite, John. 1984. *Corporate Crime in the Pharmaceutical Industry.* London: Routledge & Kegan Paul.

Brown, Michael S., Barbara G. Kelley and James Gutensohn. 1988. "A Pilot Outreach Program for Small Quantity Generators of Hazardous Waste." *American Journal of Public Health* 78: 1343–346.

Campbell, Janeth A. 1988. *State Hazardous Waste Management and Pollution Prevention Programs in Florida.* Tallahassee: Florida Department of Environmental Regulation.

Center for Hazardous Materials Research [CHMR]. 1987. *Hazardous Waste Minimization Manual for Small Quantity Generators in Pennsylvania.* Pittsburgh.

Cera, David, Kevin McDonald, Cindy McComas, Dan Reinke and LeAllen Estrem. 1988. *Hazardous and Industrial Waste Programs 1988 Evaluation Report.* Roseville: Minnesota Pollution Control Agency.

Clark, D. G. 1966. *The Industrial Manager—His Background and Career Pattern.* London: Business Publications.

Clinard, Marshall B., Peter C. Yeager, Jeanne Brissette, David Petrashek and Elizabeth Harries. 1979. *Illegal Corporate Behavior.* Washington, D.C.: National Institute of Law Enforcement and Criminal Justice.

Clinard Marshall B. and Peter C. Yeager. 1980. *Corporate Crime.* New York: Free Press.

Coase, Ronald. 1960. "The Problem of Social Cost." *Journal of Law and Economics* 3 (October): 1–44.

Cohn, Theodore and Roy A. Lindberg. 1974. *Survival and Growth: Management Strategies for Small Firms.* New York: American Management Association.

Cook, Brian J. 1988. *Bureaucratic Politics and Regulatory Reform: The EPA and Emissions Trading.* New York: Greenwood Press.

Cook, Thomas D. and Donald T. Campbell. 1979. *Quasi-Experimentation Design and Analysis for Field Settings.* Boston: Houghton Mifflin Company.

Cooley, Philip C. and Charles E. Edwards. 1983. "Financial Objectives of Small Firms." *American Journal of Small Business* 8 (July-September): 27–31.

Copeman, George. 1955. *Leaders of British Industry.* London: Gee & Company.

Cox, D. R. 1970. *Analysis of Binary Data*. London: Chapman & Hill.

Cyert, Richard M., Herbert A. Simon, and Donald B. Trow. 1956. "Observation of a Business Decision." *Journal of Business* 29: 237–48.

Cyert, Richard M., and James G. March. 1963. *A Behavioral Theory of the Firm*. Englewood Cliffs, N.J.: Prentice-Hall.

Dandridge, Thomas C. and Murphy A. Sewall. 1978. "A Priority Analysis of the Problems of Small Business Managers." *American Journal of Small Business* 2: 28–36.

Dauphin, Jeffrey, William Stough, Alice Tomboulian, Lillian Dean, Timothy Westerdake and Mike Dawkins. 1984. *Investigations and Recommendations for a Management System for Small Quantities of Hazardous Waste from Michigan Business and Industry*. Lansing: Michigan Department of Natural Resources.

Dearborn, D. C. and H. A. Simon. 1958. "Selective Perception: The Identifications of Executives." *Sociometry* 21: 140–44.

Deeks, John. 1976. *The Small Firm Owner-Manager: Entrepreneurial Behavior and Management Practice*. New York: Praeger Publishers.

Deyle, Robert E. 1985. "Source Reduction by Hazardous Waste Generating Firms in New York State." Syracuse, N.Y.: Syracuse University Technology and Information Policy Program Working Paper No. 85–010.

DiMento, Joseph F. 1986. *Environmental Law and American Business*. New York: Plenum Press.

Diver, Colin S. 1980. "A Theory of Regulatory Enforcement." *Public Policy* 28: 261–75.

Drayton, William. 1980. "Economic Law Enforcement." *Harvard Environmental Law Review* 4: 1–40.

Ehrlich, Isaac. 1974. "Participation in Illegitimate Activities: An Economic Analysis." In *Essays in the Economics of Crime and Punishment*, Gary S. Becker and William M. Landes, eds. New York: Columbia University Press.

Einhorn, Hillel J. and Robin M. Hogarth. 1982. "Behavioral Decision Theory: Processes of Judgment and Choice." In *Decision Making: An Interdisciplinary Inquiry*, Gerardo R. Ungson and Daniel N. Braunstein, eds. Boston: Kent Publishing Company.

Environmental Resources Management, Inc. [ERM]. 1985. *Hazardous Waste Facilities Need Assessment: Appendix D—Small Quantity Generator Study*. Albany: New York State Department of Environmental Conservation.

Finegan, Jay. 1986. "Down in the Dumps." *INC* (September): 64–68.

Fisse, Brent and John Braithwaite. 1983. *The Impact of Publicity on Corporate Offenders*. Albany: State University of New York Press.

Florida Department of Environmental Regulation [FDER]. 1988. *Report to the Governor and Cabinet: Progress Report on the Needs Assessment for Hazardous Waste Management*. Tallahassee.

Francis, Joe D. and Lawrence Busch. 1975. "What We Now Know About 'I Don't Knows'." *Public Opinion Quarterly* 39: 207–18.

Freeman, Myrick A., Robert H. Haveman and Allen V. Kneese. 1973. *The Economics of Environmental Policy*. New York: John Wiley & Sons.

Gashlin, Kevin. New Jersey Department of Environmental Protection, Hazardous Waste Advisement Program. 1986. Personal communication, January 22.

Geis, Gilbert. 1967. "The Heavy Electrical Equipment Antitrust Cases of 1961." In *Criminal Behavior Systems*, Marshall Clinard and Richard Quinney, eds. New York: Holt, Rinehart and Winston.

———. 1982. *On White-Collar Crime*. Lexington, Mass.: Lexington Books.

Ghassemi, Masood, K. Yu, K. Crawford, B. Edmondson, S. Quinlivan and R. Scofield. 1979. *Technical Environment Impacts of Various Approaches for Regulating Small Volume Hazardous Waste Generators. Volume I: Technical Analysis*. Washington, D.C.: U.S. Environmental Protection Agency.

Ghassemi, Masood, Sandra Quinlivan and Michael Powers. 1980. "Small Volume Hazardous Waste Generators." *Environmental Science and Technology* 14: 786–90.

Gibbs, Jack P. 1975. *Crime, Punishment, and Deterrence*. New York: Elsevier Scientific Publishing Company.

Grasmick, Harold G. and Lynn Appleton. 1977. "Legal Punishments and Social Stigma: A Comparison of Two Deterrence Models." *Social Science Quarterly* 58 (June): 15–28.

Greer, Charles R. and H. Kirk Downey. 1982. "Industrial Compliance with Social Legislation: Investigations of Decision Rationales." *Academy of Management Review* 7: 488–98.

Grisham, Joe W. 1986. *Health Aspects of the Disposal of Waste Chemicals*. New York: Pergamon Press.

Hawkins, Keith. 1984. *Environment and Enforcement Regulation and the Social Definition of Pollution*. Oxford, England: Clarendon Press.

Hill, Chris, Marc D. Jones and Edgar Berkey. 1984. *Compliance Assistance Activities for Small Quantity Generators of Hazardous Waste*. Washington, D.C.: U.S. Environmental Protection Agency Small Businness Ombudsman.

ICF Incorporated. 1983. *Small Business Pollution Control Equipment Financing: An Assessment of Federal Assistance Programs*. Washington, D.C.: U.S. Environmental Protection Agency.

Industrial Economics, Inc. 1985. *Regulatory Analysis for Proposed Regulations Under RCRA for Small Quantity Generators of Hazardous Waste*. Washington, D.C.: U.S. Environmental Protection Agency.

Jacob, Herbert. 1980. "Deterrent Effects of Formal and Informal Sanctions." In *Policy Implementation: Penalties or Incentives*, John Brigham and Don W. Brown, eds. Beverly Hills, Calif.: Sage Publications.

Jones, Marc D. 1984. "Regulatory Education Program for Small Quantity Hazardous Waste Generators in the United States." Presented at the Hazwaste '84 Forum. Washington, D.C.: U.S. Environmental Protection Agency, Small Business Ombudsman Office, June 14.

Jones, Ralpah T. and Gene E. Fax. 1984a. *A Study of State Programs for the Regulation of Small Quantity Generators of Hazardous Waste. Draft Final Report.. Volume 1: Analysis of State Programs*. Washington, D.C.: U.S. Environmental Protection Agency.

———. 1984b. *A Study of State Programs for the Regulation of Small Quantity*

Generators of Hazardous Waste. Draft Final Report. Volume 2: Case Studies. Washington, D.C.: U.S. Environmental Protection Agency.

Josephon, Julian. 1984. "Small-Quantity Waste Generators." *Environmental Science and Technology* 18: 155A–156A.

Kadish, Sanford H. 1963. "Some Observations on the Use of Criminal Sanctions in Enforcing Economic Regulations." *Chicago Law Review* 30 (Spring): 423–49.

Katz, Marvin G. 1988. "Muddy Waters For Small Generators." *Waste Age* (September): 64–65, 68, 72, 74, 76.

Kleman, Jan. Florida Department of Environmental Regulation, Hazardous Waste Management Section. 1988. Personal communication, December.

Klosky, Kenneth, Frank Arnold, Sudhakar Kesavan, Pamela Bridgen, Dan Francke, A. C. Barker, Christopher Lough, Jean Williams and Edward Conway. 1985. *Economic Analysis of Resource Conservation and Recovery Act Regulations for Small Quantity Generators.* Washington, D.C.: U.S. Environmental Protection Agency.

Kneese Allen V. and Blair T. Bower. 1979. *Environmental Quality and Residuals Management.* Baltimore: Johns Hopkins University Press.

Kovel, Alexander. 1969. "A Case for Civil Penalties: Air Pollution Control." *Journal of Urban Law* 46: 153–71.

Kramer, Ronald C. 1982. "Corporate Crime: An Organizational Perspective." In *White-Collar and Economic Crime Multidisciplinary and Cross-National Perspectives*, Peter Wickman and Timothy Dailey, eds. Lexington, Mass.: Lexington Books.

Kriesberg, Simeon M. 1976. "Decisionmaking Models and the Control of Corporate Crime." *Yale Law Journal* 85 (July): 1091–129.

Krislov, Samuel. 1972. "The Perimeters of Power: The Concept of Compliance as an Approach to the Study of the Legal and Political Processes." In *Compliance and the Law: A Multi-Disciplinary Approach*, Samuel Krislov, Keith O. Boyum, Jerry N. Clark, Roger C. Shaefer and Susan O. White, eds. Beverly Hills, Calif.: Sage Publications.

Kunreuther, Howard. 1976. "Limited Knowledge and Insurance Protection." *Public Policy* 24: 227–61.

———. 1982. "The Economics of Protection Against Low Probability Events." In *Decision Making: An Interdisciplinary Inquiry*, Gerardo R. Ungson and Daniel N. Braunstein, eds. Boston: Kent Publishing Company.

Lane, Robert E. 1966. *The Regulation of Businessmen.* Hamden, Conn.: Archon Books.

Leonard, William N. and Marvin Glenn Weber. 1970. "Automakers and Dealers: A Study of Criminogenic Market Forces." *Law and Society Review* 4 (February): 407–24.

Levin, Michael H. 1982. "Getting There: Implementing the 'Bubble' Policy," In *Social Regulation: Strategies for Reform*, Eugene Bardach and Robert A. Kagan, eds. San Francisco: Institute for Contemporary Studies.

Levinson, Alfred and John Koskowitz. 1988. "The Impact of Hazardous Waste Policy on Small Business." *Hazardous Waste and Hazardous Materials* 5: 267–273.

Linder, Stephen H. and Mark E. McBride. 1984. "Enforcement Costs and Regulatory Reform: The Agency and Firm Response." *Journal of Environmental Economics and Management* 11: 327–46.

March, James G. and Zur Shapira. 1982. "Behavioral Decision Theory and Organizational Decision Theory." In *Decision Making: An Interdisciplinary Inquiry*, Gerardo R. Ungson and Daniel N. Braunstein, eds. Boston: Kent Publishing Company.

Marcus, Alfred A. 1980. "Command and Control: An Assessment of Smokestack Emission Regulation." In *Policy Implementation: Penalties or Incentives*, John Brigham and Don W. Brown, eds. Beverly Hills, Calif.: Sage Publications.

Marten, Bradley M. 1981. "Regulation of the Transportation of Hazardous Materials: A Critique and a Proposal." *Harvard Environmental Law Review* 5: 345–76.

McMillan, Charles J. 1980. "Qualitative Models of Organizational Decision-Making." *Journal of General Management* 5: 22–39.

Meiorin, Emy Chan. 1988. *Toxics Away! The Alameda County Pilot Collection Program for Small Quantity Generators of Hazardous Waste*. Oakland, Calif.: Association of Bay Area Governments.

Miles, Robert H. 1980. *Macro Organizational Behavior*. Oakland, N.J.: Scott, Foresman & Company.

Miller, Dorothy, Ann Rosenthal, Don Miller and Sheryl Ruzek. 1971. "Public Knowledge of Criminal Penalties: A Research Report." In *Theories of Punishment*, Stanley Grupp, ed. Bloomington: Indiana University Press.

Minnesota Technical Assistance Program. 1986. *A Year of Service: Minnesota Technical Assistance Program 1985 Annual Report*. Minneapolis.

Minnesota Waste Management Board. 1986. *Hazardous Waste Programs Evaluation Report*. Crystal.

Mueller, Fred J. 1963. *The Burden of Compliance: A Study of the Nature and Cost of Tax Collection by the Small Business Firm*. Washington, D.C.: U.S. Small Business Administration.

Nagel, Stuart S. 1974. "Incentives for Compliance with Environmental Law." *American Behavioral Scientist* 17 (May/June): 690–710.

Nagin, Daniel. 1978. "General Deterrence: A Review of the Empirical Evidence." In *Deterrence and Incapacitation: Estimating the Effects of Criminal Sanctions on Crime Rates*, Alfred Blumstein, Jacqueline Cohen and Daniel Nagin, eds. Washington, D.C.: National Academy of Sciences.

National Economic Development Office. 1965. *Management Recruitment and Development*. London: H.M.S.O.

National Transportation Safety Board [NTSB]. 1979. *Noncompliance with Hazardous Materials Safety Regulations*. Washington, D.C.

Nemeth, John C. and Kevin L. Kamperman. 1985. *The Georgia Tech Hazardous Waste On-Site Consultation Program: Approach and Results*. Atlanta: Georgia Institute of Technology.

———. 1986. *The Georgia Tech Hazardous Waste On-Site Consultation Program: 1985 Final Report*. Atlanta: Georgia Institute of Technology.

Newman, Donald J. 1958. "White-Collar Crime: An Overview and Analysis." *Law and Contemporary Problems* 23 (Autumn): 735–53.

New York State Environmental Facilities Corporation. 1987. *Sixth Annual Report Industrial Materials Recycling Program.* Albany.

O'Brien, Turlough. 1978. "The Use of Civil Penalties in Enforcing the Clean Water Act Amendments of 1977." *University of San Francisco Law Review* 12 (Spring): 437–63.

Office of Technology Assessment [OTA]. 1986. *Serious Reduction of Hazardous Waste.* Washington, D.C.

Packer, Herbert L. 1968. *The Limits of the Criminal Sanction.* Stanford, Calif.: Stanford University Press.

Page, Edward C., Jr. and Paul A. Ellsworth. 1983. "Environmental Compliance Audits for Small Businesses in Massachusetts First Step to Hazardous Waste Source Reduction." In *Massachusetts Hazardous Waste Source Reduction Conference Proceedings*, Redmond Clark, ed. Boston: Massachusetts Department of Environmental Management, Bureau of Solid Waste Disposal.

Palmer, Edward, Robert Deyle, John Kohn, Alan Rabideau and Ronald Scrudato. 1986. *A Feasibility Study for Establishing a New York State Research and Development Center for Hazardous Waste Management.* Albany, N.Y.: Rockefeller Institute of Government.

Paternoster, Raymond, Linda E. Saltzman, Gordon P. Waldo, and Theodore G. Chiricos. 1982. "Causal Ordering in Deterrence Research: An Examination of the Perceptions—Behavior Relationship." In *Deterrence Reconsidered Methodological Innovations*, John Hagan, ed. Beverly Hills, Calif.: Sage Publications.

Peterson, Robert A. 1984. "Small Business Management Assistance: Needs and Sources." *American Journal of Small Business* 2: 34–45.

Phifer, Russell W. and William R. McTigue. 1988. *Handbook of Hazardous Waste Management for Small Quantity Generators.* Chelsea, Mich.: Lewis Publishers.

Pindyck, Robert S. and Daniel L. Rubenfeld. 1981. *Econometric Models and Economic Forecasts.* New York: McGraw-Hill.

Polinsky, A. Mitchell and Steven Shavell. 1979. "The Optimal Tradeoff Between the Probability and Magnitude of Fines." *American Economic Review* 69 (December): 880–91.

Porter, J. Winston. 1987. "Dr. J. Winston Porter's Address at HWHM–87." *Focus* (April): 1–2.

Rapoport, Ronald B. 1979. "What They Don't Know Can Hurt You." *American Journal of Political Science* 23: 805–15.

Rebovich, Donald J. 1986. "Exploring Hazardous Waste Crime Characteristics: An Examination of Four Northeastern States." Paper presented at the Annual Conference of the American Society of Criminology. Atlanta, Ga.: October 30.

Rice, George H. and Richard E. Hamilton. 1979. "Decision Theory and the Small Businessman." *American Journal of Small Business* 4 (July): 1–9.

Roberts, Marc J. and Jeremy S. Bluhm. 1981. *The Choices of Power.* Cambridge, Mass.: Harvard University Press.

Robinson, Richard B. and John A. Pearce. 1984. "Research Thrusts in Small Firm Strategic Planning." *Academy of Management Review* 9: 128–37.

Rodricks, Joseph V. 1984. "Risk Assessment at Hazardous Waste Disposal Sites." *Hazardous Waste* 1 (3): 333–62.

Rood, R. Fenton, Director Solid Waste Division, Oklahoma State Department of Health. 1988. Personal communication, August.

Ruder, Eric, Richard Wells, Michael Battaglia and Richard Anderson. 1985. *National Small Quantity Hazardous Waste Generator Survey.* Washington, D.C.: U.S. Environmental Protection Agency.

Ruhl, J. B. 1988. "De Minimis Settlement Policy Leaves Small Volume Contributors Guessing." *Natural Resources and Environment* 3 (1): 35–36.

Russell, Lorene Jackson. 1985. *Alternative Disposal Programs for Small Quantities of Hazardous Waste.* Oakland, Calif.: Association of Bay Area Governments.

——— and Emy Chan Meiorin. 1985. *The Disposal of Hazardous Waste by Small Quantity Generators: Magnitude of the Problem.* San Francisco: Association of Bay Area Governments.

Sabatier, Paul A. and Daniel A. Mazmanian. 1981. "The Implementation of Public Policy: A Framework of Analysis." In *Effective Policy Implementation,* Daniel A. Mazmanian and Paul A. Sabatier, eds. Lexington, Mass.: Lexington Books.

SAS Institute, Inc. 1986. *SUGI Supplemental Library User's Guide* 5 Ed. Cary, N.C.

Schecter, Roger N. 1987a. "Reduction of Hazardous Wastes: Innovative Opportunities for Industry and Government." Paper presented at the Government Institutes, Inc. Waste Minimization Conference. Washington, D.C.: February 19–20.

———. 1987b. "Summary of State Waste Reduction Efforts." Photocopy of unpublished report, March.

Scholz, John T. 1984a. "Reliability, Responsiveness, and Regulatory Policy." *Public Administration Review* (March/April): 145–53.

———. 1984b. "Voluntary Compliance and Regulatory Enforcement." *Law & Policy* (October): 385–404.

Schwartz, Seymour I., Wendy Pratt Cuckovich, Nancy Steffenson Ostrom and Cecilia F. Cox. 1987. *Managing Hazardous Wastes Produced by Small Quantity Generators.* Sacramento: Senate Office of Research, California Legislature.

Shuman, Jeffrey C. 1975. "Corporate Planning in Small Companies—A Survey." *Long Range Planning* 8: 81–90.

Simon, Herbert A. 1955. "A Behavioral Model of Rational Choice." *Quarterly Journal of Economics* 69: 99–118.

———. 1959. "Theories of Decision-Making in Economics and Behavioral Science." *American Economic Review* 49: 253–83.

———. 1972. "Theories of Bounded Rationality." In *Decision and Organization,* C. B. Radner and R. Radner, eds. Amsterdam: North Holland Publishing Company.

———. 1976. *Administrative Behavior,* 3d ed. New York: Free Press.

———. 1979. "Rational Decision Making in Business Organizations." *American Economic Review* 69 (September): 493–513.

Sloan, William M., Gary Hunt and Richard Walters. 1983. "An Approach to

Technical Assistance for Industrial and Hazardous Waste Generators." In *Massachusetts Hazardous Waste Source Reduction Conference*, Redmond Clark, ed. Boston: Massachusetts Department of Environmenntal Management, Bureau of Solid Waste Disposal.

Slovic, Paul, Baruch Fischhoff, Sarah Lichtenstein, Bernard Corrigan and Barbara Combs. 1977. "Preference for Insuring Against Probable Small Losses: Insurance Implications." *Journal of Risk and Insurance* 44: 237–58.

Smaller Business Association of New England [SBANE]. 1983. *SBANE Hazardous Waste Survey: Executive Summary*. Boston.

Smith, B. P. 1987. "Exposure and Risk Assessment." In *Hazardous Waste Management Engineering*, Edward J. Martin and James H. Johnson, Jr., eds. New York: Van Nostrand Reinhold.

Snow, Harold E. 1988a. *Summary Report Small Quantity Generator Waste Audit Project*. Albany, N.Y.: NYS Environmental Facilities Corporation.

———. 1988b. *Waste Management Audit Results: Onondaga County Small Quantity Generators: An EPA Funded Program*. Albany, N.Y.: NYS Environmental Facilities Corporation.

Sommers, Paul and Roland J. Cole. 1981. "Costs of Compliance and Medium-Sized Businesses." *American Journal of Small Business* 6: 25–33.

Southern California Association of Governments. 1985. *North Hollywood Pilot Project: Hazardous Waste Management Plan for Small-Quantity Generators Final Report*. Los Angeles.

Steger, Wilbur A., Nazir G. Dossani, Deborah Elcock, Deborah Seltzer and Stephen D. Sinclair. 1983. *Environmental Regulations and Small Businesses: An Overview of Issues Concerning the Economic Impact of EPA Regulations on Small Businesses*. Washington, D.C.: U.S. Environmental Protection Agency.

Stigler, George J. 1970. "The Optimum Enforcement of Laws." *Journal of Political Economy* 78 (May/June): 526–36.

Stone, Alan F. 1982. *Regulation and Its Alternatives*. Washington, D.C.: Congressional Quarterly Press.

Stover, Robert V. and Don W. Brown. 1975. "Understanding Compliance and Noncompliance with Law: The Contributions of Utility Theory." *Social Science Quarterly* (December): 363–75.

Sutherland, Edwin H. 1949. *White Collar Crime*. New York: Holt, Rinehart & Winston.

Tittle, Charles R. 1980. *Sanctions and Social Deviance: The Question of Deterrence*. New York: Praeger.

United States Chamber of Commerce [USCOC]. 1982. "Survey on Regulation." *Washington Report* (August 3).

United States Environmental Protection Agency [EPA]. 1980. *Federal Register* 45 (May 19): 33221.

———. 1985. *Does Your Business Produce Hazardous Wastes? Many Small Businesses Do*. EPA/530–SW–010. Washington, D.C.

———. 1986a. *Understanding the Small Quantity Generator Hazardous Waste Rules: A Handbook for Small Business*. EPA/530–SW–86–019. Washington, D.C.

———. 1986b. *Report to Congress: Minimization of Hazardous Waste.* Vol. 1. EPA/530–SW–86–033A. Washington, D.C.

———. 1987a. *Federal Register* 52 (June 30): 24333.

———. 1987b. *Federal Register* 52 (November 12): 43393.

———. 1988A. *The Solid Waste Dilemma: An Agenda for Action.* Washington, D.C.

———. 1988b. "RCRA Integrated Training and Technical Assistance Program; Financial Assistance Program; Availability for Review." *Federal Register* 53 (January 22): 1836.

———. 1988c. *Federal Register* 53 (February 11): 4070.

———. 1988d. "Hazardous Substance Research Centers; Solicitation for Applications." *Federal Register* 53 (March 22): 9358.

———. 1988e. *Federal Register* 53 (June 2): 20165.

———. 1988f. "Financial Assistance Program Eligible for Review." *Federal Register* 53 (July 18): 27077.

———. 1988g. "Solid Waste Disposal Facility Criteria." *Federal Register* 53 (August 30): 33314.

———. Small Business Ombudsman [EPASBO]. 1984. *Assistance Programs for Pollution Control Financing.* Washington, D.C.

———. Small Business Task Group [SBTG]. 1984. *EPA Small Business Initiatives—Strategy for Improved Regulation and Compliance.* Washington, D.C.: September 28.

United States General Accounting Office [GAO]. 1983. *Information on Disposal Practices of Generators of Small Quantities of Hazardous Waste.* Washington, D.C.

———. 1988. *Hazardous Waste: Many Enforcement Actions Do Not Meet EPA Standards.* Washington, D.C.

Van Hoorn, T. P. 1979. "Strategic Planning in Small and Medium-Sized Companies." *Long Range Planning* 12: 84–91.

Viscusi, W. Kip and Richard J. Zeckhauser. 1979. "Optimal Standards with Incomplete Enforcement." *Public Policy* 27 (Fall): 437–56.

Welsh, John A. and Jerry F. White. 1981. "A Small Business is not a Little Big Business." *Harvard Business Review* 57: 18–19.

Westat, Inc. 1984. *National Survey of Hazardous Facilities Regulated Under RCRA in 1981.* Washington, D.C.: U.S. Environmental Protection Agency.

Witte, Ann D. and Diane F. Woodbury. 1983. "What We Know About the Factors Affecting Compliance with Tax Laws." In *Income Tax Compliance: A Report of the ABA Section of Taxation Invitational Conference on Income Tax Compliance*, Phillip Sawicki, ed. Reston, Va.: American Bar Association.

Wu, Jy S., Helene Hilger and Mary McDaniel. 1984. "Waste Management for Small Quantity Generators in North Carolina." Paper presented at National AIChE Symposium on Advanced Technology and Waste Treatment, Philadelphia.

Index

Acids and alkalies, 7

Airline industry, 57

Air quality regulations, compliance, 42–43

Alameda County, California, collection route service program, 102–3, 106–8

Apprehension: probability of, 32, 34, 42; actual, in New Jersey, 87; actual, in U.S., 87; estimates of, by smaller generators, 74, 86–87, 91, 108; as factor, in compliance decisions, 44, 85, 108–9; salience to smaller generators, 87, 108

Association of Bay Area Governments (ABAG), California: collection route service program, 102–3, 106–8; survey of smaller generators, 12, 65, 103

Automotive repair and body shops, 3, 46, 52, 102. *See also* Vehicle maintenance

California: regulation of smaller generators, 10, 102–3; smaller generator program, 94, 97, 100; waste management by smaller generators, 12

California State Department of Health Services, 97

California State Senate, smaller generator study, 94, 108

Cannons Engineering Corporation, de minimis settlement under CERCLA, 57

Center for Hazardous Materials Research (CHMR), University of Pittsburgh: hazardous waste minimization manual, 94; waste audit program, 13

Ceramics industry, 3

CERCLA. *See* Comprehensive Environmental Response, Compensation and Liability Act

Command-and-control regulation, 1–2,

ABOUT THE AUTHOR

ROBERT E. DEYLE is a research fellow in the Science and Public Policy Program at the University of Oklahoma and an assistant professor of civil engineering and environmental science.

ABOUT THE CONTRIBUTOR

ROSEMARY O'LEARY is an assistant professor of public and environmental affairs at Indiana University.